ANXIOUS ATTACHMENT WORKBOOK

Your Guide to Transforming Relationship Fears into Confidence and Security in Life and Love - Anxious Attachment Recovery

Copyright 2023 - Yevhenii Lozovyi - All rights reserved.

The content contained within this book may not be reproduced, duplicated, or transmitted without direct written permission from the author or the publisher.

Under no circumstances will any blame or legal responsibility be held against the publisher or author for any damages, reparation, or monetary loss due to the information contained within this book, either directly or indirectly.

Legal Notice:
This book is copyright-protected and is only for personal use. You cannot amend, distribute, sell, use, quote, or paraphrase any part or the content within this book without the consent of the author or publisher.

Disclaimer Notice:
Please note the information contained within this document is for educational and entertainment purposes only. All effort has been executed to present accurate, up-to-date, reliable, and complete information. No warranties of any kind are declared or implied. Readers acknowledge that the author is not engaged in rendering legal, financial, medical, or professional advice. The content within this book has been derived from various sources. Please consult a licensed professional before attempting any techniques outlined in this book.

By reading this document, the reader agrees that the author is under no circumstances responsible for any direct or indirect losses incurred as a result of using the information contained within it, including, but not limited to, errors, omissions, or inaccuracies.

ISBN Print: 978-1-962027-26-7
ISBN Kindle: 978-1-962027-24-3

A Note from The Author

I hope this book will benefit you in your journey to increase your happiness and quality of life!

If you have not claimed your bonus exercise manuals, do not hesitate to email with a request. They will help you on your journey!

Note: *How to request additional exercise manuals*

Email *the subject line:* *The Book Title + exercises request.*

I do not spam! I only strive to provide value. For example, I only email monthly with a free Kindle book offer when Amazon allows me to schedule a promotion. Many books are in work now, and if you find the subject interesting, you will have a chance to receive the Kindle version for free. My main interests are mental and physical health, biohacking, and everything else that can increase happiness and quality of life.

Constructive criticism is always welcome! I am always looking for ways to improve the quality and accessibility of the materials. Feel free to reach out to

yevhenii@fiolapublishing.com

If you find this book helpful and could benefit others, please leave a review on Amazon. It would mean a word to me if you do so.

Best wishes,

Yevhenii

Table of Contents

Introduction to Your Transformation Journey 1
    Understanding Attachment Theory 1
    Attachment Theory's Ten Core Principles 2
    The Role of Emotional Intelligence in Nurturing Relationships 8
    Overview of Attachment Styles 9
    Workbook Structure and Effective Use 13

Chapter 1: Understanding Anxious Attachment 15
    Defining Anxious Attachment 15
    Origins of Anxious Attachment 17
    Anxious Attachment in Adult Relationships 19
    Deep Dive: The Science Behind Anxious Attachment 21
    Neurological Perspectives on Attachment 22
    Practical Implications: Navigating Emotional Regulation 24
    Psychological Perspectives on Attachment 25
    Fear and Insecurity in Anxious Attachment 27
    Making the Science Actionable 29
    Impact on Personal and Professional Life 31

    Chapter Exercises : Anxious Attachment Self-Assessment Quiz 33
    Journaling Prompts on Attachment History 35
    Trigger Mapping Exercise Guide 36
    Emotional Response Diary Guide 38
    Identifying Needs and Desires in Relationships 39

Chapter 2: The Role of Emotional Intelligence in Relationships 43
    Introduction to Emotional Intelligence (EQ) 43
    EQ and Anxious Attachment 46
    Developing EQ to Improve Relationship Dynamics 47

    Chapter Exercises: Empathetic Validation Exercise 50
    Letter to Your Future Self-Exercise 52
    Challenging Insecure Thoughts Exercise 53

Rejection Processing Exercise 55
Empathy Mapping Exercise 57

Chapter 3: Identifying Anxious Behaviors in Relationships 61
Common Behaviors and Patterns Associated with Anxious Attachment 62
Introduction to Techniques for Managing Anxious Behaviors 64
Mindfulness Practices 65
Journaling 67
Cognitive-Behavioral Techniques 68
Building a Toolkit for Change 69
Identifying Triggers and Emotional Responses 70

Chapter Exercises: Anxious Attachment Behavior Log Exercise 73
Anxiety Management Techniques Exercise 74
Fear Facing Exercise 77
Secure Attachment Role Models Exercise 79

Chapter 4: Building Self-Awareness 83
The Importance of Self-Awareness in Overcoming Anxious Attachment 84
Section 1: Exploring Personal History and Beliefs 84
Life Timeline Exercise: Understanding Your Attachment Style 85
Understanding Your Belief Systems 87
Core Values Clarification Exercise: Aligning Personal Values with Behaviors 87
Belief System Mapping: Core Beliefs About Relationships 89
Section 2: The Roots of Anxious Attachment 91
Exercise: Reflective Prompts to Explore Early Memories of Anxiety and Fear in Relationships 91
Section 3: Mindfulness and Self-Awareness 93
Mindfulness Meditation for Awareness: Enhancing Self-Awareness Through Guided Practice 94
Section 4: Strategies for Self-Compassion 95
Self-Compassion Letters: Writing to Oneself in Times of Stress or Self-Doubt 98
Section 5: Integrating Self-Awareness into Daily Life 99
Daily Self-Reflection Prompts: Fostering Deeper Self-Awareness 100
Emotion Body Mapping: Identifying Physical Manifestations of Emotions 102

Chapter 5: Cultivating Secure Attachment from Within ... 105
Steps to Internalize the Qualities of Secure Attachment ... 107
Emotional Regulation ... 108
Resilience in the Face of Adversity ... 110
Techniques for Reprogramming Old Beliefs and Patterns ... 112
Fostering Secure Attachment Skills (SAS) ... 113

Chapter Exercises: Secure Attachment Visualization Exercise Manual ... 117
Self-Reliance Challenges Exercise Manual ... 119
Resilience Building Activities Exercise Manual ... 122
Reprogramming Negative Beliefs Exercise Manual ... 124
Positive Affirmation Practice Exercise Manual ... 125

Chapter 6: Understanding Conflict in the Context of Anxious Attachment ... 129
Step-by-Step Blueprint for Constructive Conflict Resolution ... 130
Real-World Examples and Role-Plays ... 137
Conclusion: The Growth Potential in Conflict ... 139

Chapter Exercises: "I Feel" Statements Exercise ... 141
Boundary Setting Workshop ... 143
Understanding without Agreeing with Exercise ... 144
The Perspective Shift Exercise ... 146
Jealousy Journaling Exercise ... 148

Introduction to Your Transformation Journey

Welcome to your transformative journey towards understanding, resilience, and enriched connections. The "Anxious Attachment Workbook" stands as your beacon, guiding you through the complexities of anxious attachment towards a horizon of confidence, security, and deeper relationship bonds. Our mission is to arm you with the necessary insights, tools, and comprehension to untangle the intricacies of attachment in adult relationships, laying down a solid foundation of self-awareness and emotional resilience. This workbook is your companion in a transformative journey that promises enhanced relationship dynamics, a profound self-understanding, and a robust emotional fortitude.

Purpose and Goals

This workbook is anchored in a deep commitment to navigate you from the stormy seas of anxious attachment to the serene waters of secure, rewarding connections. Our objective extends beyond shedding light on your path; it includes walking beside you as you apply the workbook's insights and strategies to your life. Our goals are comprehensive: to unlock a deeper self-understanding and awareness of your attachment style, to furnish you with emotional regulation tools, and to boost your empathy and connectivity skills. Our vision is for you to conclude this journey with an empowered self-identity, strengthened relationships, and the resilience to confidently tackle life's adversities.

Understanding Attachment Theory

At its essence, attachment theory investigates how our earliest relationships shape our emotional development and influence our adult bonds. It serves as a lens through which we can examine our relationship patterns and behaviors. Anxious attachment, marked by an intense fear of abandonment, overwhelming emotional responses, and a continuous quest for validation, can significantly impact one's self-esteem and relationship dynamics. This workbook provides clarity and guidance for those eager to comprehend and alter these patterns, offering a path to understanding and transformation.

Embracing Emotional Intelligence

Emotional Intelligence (EQ) is pivotal in personal evolution and nurturing healthy relationships. It involves the ability to identify, comprehend, and manage our emotions and empathize with others. For those wrestling with anxious attachment, cultivating a high EQ is like learning a new dialect that facilitates expressing needs, fears, and desires in ways that encourage connection and understanding rather than conflict and alienation. This workbook is your guide to enhancing your EQ, equipping you with the ability to more effectively manage anxious attachment challenges and cultivate deeper, more fulfilling connections.

The Roots of Attachment in Adult Love

Attachment isn't just for babies and their caregivers; it's a lifelong need. Originated by John Bowlby and later applied to adult relationships, attachment theory helps explain why we act like we do in love. Are you clingy, distant, or maybe a mix of both? Understanding your attachment style can be the first step in resolving the issues that keep you both up at night.

So, as you go through this journey, remember that understanding the science isn't just for therapists and academics. It's for anyone who wants an emotionally fulfilling and enduring relationship.

Attachment Theory's Ten Core Principles

1. *The Lifelong Urge to Connect: Attachment as a Basic Human Need.*

Hey, let's talk about the elephant in the room—dependency. Society often paints it as a weakness. Well, surprise! Attachment theory says dependency is completely natural and crucial for healthy relationships. It's not something you grow out of, like a childhood phase. The need to connect with people you care about isn't a sign of weakness; it's the "heartbeat" of any close relationship. So when you fear losing each other, know it's a universal experience. A basic part of being human makes us social creatures at our core.

2. *The Balance of Independence and Dependence: Two Sides of the Same Coin.*

Have you ever heard you should be "completely independent" in a relationship? Well, that's a myth. According to attachment theory, there's no such thing as complete independence or over-dependence. Instead, secure dependency and autonomy are like two peas in a pod—complementing each other. When you're securely attached, you feel more confident and independent. This sense of secure connection allows you to be authentic while still being a united couple. Research shows that secure attachment enhances your sense of self (Mikulincer, 1995). In other words, belonging to someone helps you become who you're meant to be.

3. Your Safe Haven: The Comfort of Attachment.

We all have moments when life gets overwhelming. When that happens, being close to someone you love feels like fresh air. That's not just poetic language; it's backed by science. Your loved one's proximity has a calming effect on your nervous system (Schore, 1994). Think of your relationship as a safe haven that shields you from life's stress and uncertainties. This emotional comfort zone is essential for your ongoing personal growth and mental well-being.

4. The Launching Pad: Secure Attachment as Your Basecamp for Exploration.

Imagine your relationship as a secure base, like the home base in a game of tag. This safe place allows you to explore the world, take risks, and be open to new experiences. A secure attachment makes you feel safe and empowers you to be adventurous and open to life's possibilities. This "home base" in your relationship enriches your ability to reflect on yourself and adapt to new challenges (Mikulincer, 1997). It's like having a co-pilot in the journey of life.

5. The Building Blocks: Emotional Accessibility and Responsiveness.

Let's be real—physical presence isn't enough. You could be sitting next to each other and yet feel worlds apart. Emotional engagement is the magic ingredient that builds and sustains a secure bond. When you're emotionally accessible and responsive to each other, you're telling your partner, "You matter to me." On the flip side, a lack of emotional responsiveness sends a message that can be devastating: "You don't matter, and we're not connected." Emotions are attachment language; they communicate your deepest needs and desires. They're the rhythm to your relationship's melody.

6. Weathering Life's Storms: Attachment Needs in Tough Times.

Life can throw curveballs, whether a stressful job, illness, or even a seemingly harmless flirtation at a party. During these times, your attachment needs for comfort and connection amplify. Think of your attachment to each other as your emotional safety net. It helps you bounce back when life tries to knock you down. So, it's natural to seek each other out when feeling vulnerable. Remember, the need for a loving connection isn't a weakness; it's your built-in mechanism for coping with life's challenges.

7. The Emotional Rollercoaster: The Phases of Separation Distress.

Feeling ignored or neglected? You're likely to go through a cycle of emotions: first anger, then clinginess, followed by depression, and eventually, detachment. Attachment theory explains these reactions as completely normal responses to feeling disconnected. So, when you find yourselves locked in a pattern of demand and withdrawal, understand it's often a cry for emotional connection. Recognizing these patterns as calls for closeness can be the first step in breaking the cycle and finding your way back to each other.

8. Coping Styles: The Limited Ways We Deal With Emotional Distance.

Have you ever wondered why some people appear clingy while others seem aloof? Attachment theory identifies two main coping strategies when emotional needs aren't met—becoming anxious and clingy or avoiding emotional engagement altogether. Both strategies can become habits that dictate how you interact with each other, often worsening your relationship woes. Recognizing these coping styles can help you understand what you're fighting about and how to break the cycle.

9. The Stories We Tell Ourselves: Working Models of Self and Other.

Each of you carries a mental script shaped by past experiences, which influences how you view yourselves and each other. These "working models" can guide your actions and reactions in your relationship. For example, if you're securely attached, you likely view yourself as lovable and your partner as reliable. But you may doubt your worth and your partner's commitment if you're insecurely attached. Understanding these narratives can reveal the emotional truths that bubble up during heated moments, helping you rewrite the script for a healthier relationship.

10. The Profound Impact of Isolation and Loss: Attachment as a Theory of Trauma.

Attachment theory is, at its heart, a theory of trauma. It recognizes that feelings of isolation and loss are deeply traumatizing. The emotional security that comes from knowing your partner will be there for you affects your relationship and well-being. Confidence in each other's reliability can be a buffer against the chronic fears and stresses that life throws your way.

Attachment theory is more than academic jargon; it's a lens through which to understand the intricate dance of love and emotional connection. Whether you find yourself stuck in a cycle of demand and withdrawal or coping with emotional distance, the principles of attachment theory can guide you toward a deeper, more satisfying relationship. So, are you ready to explore these ideas and put them into practice? Because understanding your emotional self can be the key to unlocking a love that lasts.

The Lifelong Dance of Attachment

The Universality of Attachment Needs: From Childhood to Adulthood
You've probably heard the saying, "Love makes the world go 'round," but have you ever considered why that is? It's all about attachment—a universal need, not just for kids. Both children and adults crave attention, emotional responsiveness, and a deep connection with their loved ones. Whether you're five or fifty, the presence of a trusted person makes life's challenges more bearable and even boosts your ability to handle stress. What's more, when your partner is emotionally available and responsive, you're not just happier—you're also better at navigating the ups and downs of your relationship.

The Transformative Power of Emotional Presence
You might become anxious and preoccupied if your partner is distant or unresponsive. Just like a child feels safer when their caregiver is near, adults, too, need that emotional security to engage with the world around them fully. This emotional rope isn't just about physical presence but also nonverbal cues. From the way you look at each other to the tender moments of physical touch like hugging or kissing, emotional presence is the glue that binds your relationship.

The Safe Haven: Your Emotional Anchor in Life's Storms
Separation from a loved one—whether it's physical or emotional—triggers distress at any age. It's why you both rejoice at each other's company, especially if you've been apart. It's why you share experiences, confide secrets, and even find yourselves thinking about how the other would react to certain events. This emotional sanctuary is what everyone seeks, from the time they're in the crib to their final days.

The Unique Characteristics of Adult Attachments
However, adult relationships do differ from parent-child bonds in a few key ways:

Mental Comfort: As adults, you can find solace in your mental representation of your partner, even when apart. Unlike children, who may need physical presence for comfort, adults can carry the image of their loved ones in their minds as a source of emotional security.

The Role of Sexuality: Sex isn't just about physical pleasure or procreation; it's an attachment behavior. Ever wonder why intimacy feels so emotionally satisfying? It's because oxytocin, often called the "cuddle hormone," is released during sexual climax. Interestingly, activities that are deeply bonding in nature, like kissing, are often avoided in situations where sex is purely transactional.

Reciprocity: While a parent-child relationship is more one-sided, with the parent providing the most emotional support, adult relationships thrive on mutual give-and-take. Each partner contributes to the emotional well-being of the relationship, making it a two-way street.

So, why is this all important? Understanding the underlying principles of attachment can offer you a roadmap for navigating the complexities of your relationship. Knowing that your attachment needs are normal can free you both to seek out the emotional connection that makes life richer and more fulfilling. After all, from the cradle to the grave, we all want someone to hold us in the dark.

The Evolution of Attachment in Adult Relationships: The Timeline and Its Implications

The Maturation of Adult Bonds: Beyond Friendship.
While the flicker of friendship may ignite the spark in a new relationship, it's often not until about two years in that the attachment flame truly starts to burn. This timeline isn't arbitrary; it suggests that your shared emotional bonds need time to mature and deepen. So, if you're in the early stages of your relationship and you're not feeling that soul-stirring attachment just yet, don't worry—you're likely still in the "stimulation mode" of friendship.

Reacting to Emotional Distance: More Than Just "Communication Issues"
Have you ever noticed how even a short emotional distance can send you both into a tailspin? That's not just a "communication problem" or a temporary hiccup in your closeness. It's

your inbuilt, adaptive response to the perceived loss of your primary emotional and physical security source. So, the next time you feel like the other is "overreacting," it might be helpful to remember that this is a natural reaction to losing your emotional anchor.

Rethinking Relationship Distress: It's Not Just About Conflict
Contrary to popular belief, marital distress or the risk of divorce doesn't primarily come from negative emotions, conflicts, or bad interactions. While those factors may be the visible signs, the root often lies in the absence of emotionally responsive interactions. The real trouble begins when you or your partner fail to meet each other's attachment needs. The emotional distance and deprivation trigger conflicts and unhappiness, not vice versa.

The Healing Power of Secure Attachment: Ending Long-Standing Arguments
The good news is that once you start responding to each other's emotional needs and cues, your bond strengthens. With a secure attachment as your base, you'll find that many of your long-standing disagreements resolve themselves naturally. And even when arguments do arise, they won't have the power to shake the foundations of your relationship.

The Constant Dance: Attachment in Everyday Interactions
In relationships, attachment isn't just an internal mindset; it's a continual dance between partners. Your attachment style doesn't just reside within you; it's reflected, influenced, and even reshaped in your interactions with your loved one. This means that attachment styles can change as you learn and grow within your relationship. And that's good news for any couple looking to improve their connection.

The Nuts and Bolts: From Emotional Reactivity to Communication Competence
Understanding attachment styles can help you make sense of your emotional triggers and reactions. It explains why one of you might become anxious and needy when the other starts pulling away. But more than just offering insights, it provides a roadmap for change. For example, secure attachment promotes effective communication and collaborative problem-solving. So, focusing on building a secure attachment can be the first step toward breaking free from destructive cycles like 'demand–withdraw.'

The Role of Emotional Intelligence in Nurturing Relationships

Emotional Intelligence (EQ) is a multifaceted capability that enables individuals to recognize, understand, manage, and positively utilize their emotions. It encompasses relieving stress, communicating effectively, empathizing with others, overcoming challenges, and defusing conflict. This comprehensive understanding of EQ highlights its importance in personal development and enhancing the quality of our relationships.

The Five Core Components of EQ

1. Self-Awareness
This involves deeply understanding one's emotions, strengths, weaknesses, values, and drivers. Self-awareness is crucial because it is the first step towards managing your emotions and understanding how they affect your thoughts and actions. In the context of anxious attachment, recognizing your emotional triggers and patterns can help you navigate through the complexities of relationships with greater clarity.

2. Self-Regulation
This pertains to managing your emotions healthily, adapting to changing circumstances, and following through on commitments. Self-regulation allows you to express your emotions appropriately and restrain impulses that might lead to conflict. For someone with anxious attachment, learning to self-regulate can prevent the escalation of negative emotions and facilitate a more balanced response to relationship dynamics.

3. Motivation
Intrinsic motivation refers to the inner drive to pursue goals for personal satisfaction rather than external rewards. High EQ involves using this motivation to persist in facing obstacles and setbacks. This component is particularly important for overcoming anxious attachment behaviors by fostering resilience and a positive outlook on personal and relationship goals.

4. Empathy
Empathy is the ability to understand and share the feelings of another. It plays a pivotal role in forming deep, meaningful relationships by fostering a sense of emotional connection and

support. Developing empathy for individuals struggling with anxious attachment can help understand partners' perspectives, leading to stronger and more secure bonds.

5. Social Skills

Effective communication and adeptness in managing relationships are essential social skills encompassed by EQ. These skills enable individuals to easily navigate social complexities, build positive relationships, and constructively resolve conflicts. Improving social skills can transform anxious attachment patterns by enhancing trust, communication, and mutual respect in relationships.

The intersection of emotional intelligence and relationships reveals a powerful pathway for transforming anxious attachment into secure, fulfilling connections. High EQ equips individuals with the tools to understand and regulate their emotions, foster empathy, and navigate social interactions effectively. As we delve deeper into this workbook, we encourage you to reflect on your EQ levels and explore strategies for developing these critical skills. You can journey towards more secure attachments and healthier, more satisfying relationships through committed practice and self-reflection.

Overview of Attachment Styles

Attachment styles are patterns of expectations, needs, and behaviors in relationships formed in response to the nature of caregiving received in childhood. These styles include a secure, anxious, and avoidant attachment. Secure attachment is characterized by confidence in the availability and support of attachment figures. Anxious attachment involves fear of abandonment and a preoccupation with the attachment figure's responsiveness. Avoidant attachment is marked by a discomfort with closeness and a tendency to maintain emotional distance from others.

Anxious Attachment

Individuals with anxious attachment often exhibit a heightened sensitivity to their partners' actions and moods, driven by a deep-seated fear of rejection or abandonment. This attachment style can lead to challenges in emotional regulation, including a persistent need for reassurance and approval from others. Anxious attachment affects adult relationships profoundly, manifesting as intense worry about relationship stability and an overwhelming desire for closeness that can sometimes push partners away.

Individuals with an anxious attachment style often exhibit:

- Remarkable generosity and attentiveness towards loved ones.
- A heightened sensitivity to perceived signs of abandonment.
- A willingness to openly express their emotions.
- A tendency to attribute their emotional states to others ("You're the reason I feel this way!").

For those with an anxious attachment, the dread of abandonment looms large. When this fear is mildly provoked, it can lead to panic. Although they seek support, their expression may inadvertently alienate those they wish to draw closer to. Their immediate response to feeling hopeless or expecting disappointment can seem exaggerated or off-putting, complicating their attempts to receive the support they urgently need.

Attachment styles are fluid, with many displaying a mix of anxious and avoidant tendencies depending on the context. Within these narratives, you may also recognize traits of significant others in your life, be they family or past or present partners.

Self-Reflection and Awareness

The upcoming segments and exercises aim to guide you in identifying and understanding your anxious patterns. Approach this chapter with an open and curious mindset about yourself and your relationships, avoiding blame or criticism. This perspective is crucial for learning about yourself and catalyzing change in unhelpful behaviors.

Experiencing Anxious Attachment

Commonalities exist among those with anxious attachments in how they experience relationships. As you peruse this section, reflect on how it resonates with your relationship dynamics. Not every detail may match your experience precisely, but where you find alignment, it may be comforting to know you're not alone in these patterns.

Anxious individuals are drawn to the concept of attachment, especially romantic, viewing it as an ideal state of mutual support and deep understanding. They yearn for a partner who intuitively understands them at their core. This longing for profound understanding is pivotal at the beginning of a relationship and is a cornerstone for pursuing a long-term bond.

Challenges may arise as the relationship solidifies. The once attentive and empathetic partner may falter, triggering deep-seated fears and doubts stemming from childhood, encapsulated in the thought, "I need them, but they will let me down." This drive for connection often leads to prioritizing the partner's needs over one's own, resulting in feelings of neglect and dissatisfaction.

Anxious moments in the relationship can feel intensely painful as if the anticipated betrayal has already occurred. This craving for support is coupled with skepticism about the partner's availability, making the desired connection seem elusive and intensifying distress.

Manifestations of an anxious attachment style include jeopardizing the relationship through ultimatums or regrettable actions driven by a desperate need to communicate one's pain. Sadly, such behaviors often push the partner further away rather than eliciting the desired support.

After the turmoil subsides and reconciliation occurs, the incident reinforces the painful belief that loved ones are unreliable. Despite this, the desire for connection persists, shadowed by the fear of being too demanding to be truly loved.

Attachment theory suggests that these patterns of interaction, both giving and demanding excessively, are learned behaviors, possibly rooted in childhood experiences where you felt compelled to cater to a caregiver's emotional needs for survival. This blueprint for love, characterized by rescuing and overreaching, becomes a familiar but challenging dynamic in adult relationships.

Reflecting on your childhood, you may recall feeling dissatisfied with the attention received from caregivers despite moments of genuine connection. This inconsistency in early experiences mirrors the frustration felt in adult relationships as dependence on a partner grows.

While no description can capture everyone's experience perfectly, those with anxious attachment traits may see reflections of themselves in the scenarios described. As you ponder your significant relationships, consider how well this description aligns with your experiences and use it as a starting point for exploration and growth.

The Dynamics of Anxious Attachment in Relationships

Individuals with an anxious attachment style often exhibit reactive behaviors when their fears are activated. These reactions are not intentional but are rather spontaneous responses to their inner turmoil. Often, they might not even recognize these habitual responses, which can manifest as critical or harsh actions during moments of stress. Such impulsivity can jeopardize the relationship, undermining their desire for a stable and nurturing connection.

Anxiously attached individuals may present seemingly contradictory behaviors. They seek support and closeness, yet when overwhelmed by their emotions, they might find it challenging to be in the presence of their partners. Relationships with those with an anxious attachment style are characterized by fluctuations—periods of generosity followed by resentment, grievances, demands, brief contentment, and then generosity.

Efforts to fulfill needs through blame, anger, guilt, or persistent complaints do not usually yield the desired closeness, and often, those engaged may not immediately realize the strain this places on their companions and the overall health of their relationship. This cycle depletes the relationship's goodwill—which is essential for overcoming challenges. While appeasement might temporarily restore harmony, if it stems from a place of pressure rather than genuine giving, it erodes the foundation of trust and mutual respect that is critical for a lasting bond. This pattern of demanding fulfillment can significantly deplete the relationship's resilience and capacity to flourish.

Understanding Your Partner's Perspective

This section is designed to offer a fresh perspective to individuals with anxious attachment styles, encouraging you to consider how your behaviors may affect your partners and the overall well-being of your relationship. It highlights the significance of empathy, effective communication, and shared understanding in nurturing a supportive and loving connection.

Being partnered with someone who exhibits anxious attachment traits might sometimes feel like dealing with a stressed customer in a support role. Such individuals often express their discontent more intensely, whether verbally or through their actions, potentially appearing overly critical or angry. This level of expressiveness can challenge the capacity to respond with empathy, leading to feelings of inundation or discouragement, especially if you're frequently receiving these expressions.

Confrontations with an anxiously attached partner can be particularly challenging due to their ability to articulate their concerns vividly, often preferring continuous dialogue over uncomfortable silences. Although these interactions may seem adversarial, there is usually an underlying desire to provide support and care. However, the immediate behavior of an anxiously attached partner can trigger one's stress responses or cast doubts on their ability to be affectionate and understanding.

Responses to this situation tend to vary; some may attempt to excessively soothe their anxiously attached partner, while others might withdraw to avoid confrontation. Neither strategy is sustainable in the long run; the former may lead to personal exhaustion without adequate self-care and boundary maintenance, while the latter could increase your partner's feelings of anxiety.

Over time, an anxiously attached partner's constant negativity and perceived insatiability can heavily strain the relationship. Frequent criticisms that such partners are overly demanding, critical, and high-maintenance can lower morale and satisfaction within the relationship, particularly during challenging times. This introductory shift aims to cultivate awareness and foster a healthier dynamic between partners, emphasizing the power of mutual compassion and understanding.

Understanding one's attachment style is pivotal in navigating and improving adult relationships. By recognizing and addressing the underlying patterns and behaviors associated with anxious attachment, individuals can work towards fostering healthier, more secure connections.

Workbook Structure and Effective Use

The 'Anxious Attachment Workbook' is meticulously designed to guide readers through a transformative journey, from understanding the fundamentals of anxious attachment to cultivating secure, fulfilling relationships. The workbook is divided into chapters, each dedicated to a specific aspect of anxious attachment and emotional intelligence, structured to progress from general concepts to specific strategies and exercises. This mix of theoretical explanations, real-life examples, and practical exercises ensures a comprehensive understanding and application of the concepts discussed.

Guidance on Using the Workbook

To maximize the benefits of this workbook, we recommend setting aside regular time for reading and reflecting on the content, completing the exercises, and journaling your insights and experiences. Engage with the workbook content progressively, allowing yourself to build on the concepts and practices as you move from one chapter to the next. Creating a conducive learning environment, free from distractions and conducive to reflection, will further enhance your engagement and learning.

> *Important Note:*
>
> *This book is designed to guide you, step by step, toward building more secure and fulfilling relationships, starting from within. Each chapter delves into specific strategies and methods rooted in the latest psychological research and practical exercises to help you apply these concepts to your life.*
>
> *It's important to note that while the chapters discuss the rationale and importance of each exercise, the detailed instructions for carrying out these exercises have been thoughtfully placed at the end of each chapter, except Chapter 4.*
>
> *This structure is intended to provide a clear, focused narrative on the theoretical aspects before moving on to the practical application, allowing you to engage deeply with the material and its implications for your personal growth and relationship enhancement.*

Maximizing Benefits

Honesty and openness are crucial in the self-reflection exercises. Approach these exercises with self-compassion and patience, especially when navigating sensitive topics. Understanding and growth are iterative processes; thus, revisiting chapters and exercises over time can deepen your insights and solidify your learning. This repeated engagement facilitates a deeper connection with the material, supporting your journey towards secure attachment and healthier relationships.

Chapter 1

Understanding Anxious Attachment

Defining Anxious Attachment

Attachment theory is at the heart of our emotional world, a psychological framework that explains how our early relationships with caregivers shape our emotional bonds in adulthood. Among the various attachment styles identified, anxious attachment emerges as a pattern characterized by intense emotional responses and a deep fear of abandonment.

Individuals with an anxious attachment style often find themselves in a perpetual state of emotional turmoil, primarily because their early experiences did not consistently meet their needs for security, understanding, and reassurance. This foundational instability fosters a chronic fear of rejection and abandonment that permeates their adult relationships.

Emotional Hyperactivation

One of the hallmark features of anxious attachment is emotional hyperactivation. This term refers to the heightened emotional responsiveness to any hint of distance or disapproval from a partner. For those with an anxious attachment style, the normal ebbs and flows of a relationship can trigger profound anxiety, leading to behaviors aimed at seeking reassurance and closeness.

This emotional rollercoaster is not merely about feeling love more deeply; it's a response to the perceived threat of losing connection, which activates intense emotions as a survival mechanism. The anxious partner may experience a cascade of thoughts and feelings that are both overwhelming and exhausting, as they are constantly on alert for signs of potential loss.

Negative Self-Image

Central to the anxious attachment experience is a negative self-image, often stemming from a belief that one is inherently unworthy of love and affection. This core insecurity drives the anxious individual to seek constant validation from their partner to soothe their doubts and fears. Unfortunately, this reliance on external reassurance can never fully compensate for the internal void of self-worth, creating a cycle of neediness and dissatisfaction.

The struggle with self-image in anxious attachment is not just about lacking confidence; it's an internalized fear that without their partner's approval, they are fundamentally flawed or unlovable. This belief system exacerbates the anxiety around relationship dynamics, making it difficult for individuals to find peace within themselves or their connections.

Preoccupation with Relationships

A preoccupation with relationships also characterizes anxious attachment. This obsessive concern manifests as constant rumination about the relationship's state, hypersensitivity to changes in the partner's mood or behavior, and an excessive need for communication and reassurance.

This preoccupation can lead to behaviors that may appear controlling or overly needy, but at their core, they are attempts to secure the bond and alleviate the fear of abandonment. Unfortunately, this intense focus on the relationship can strain partnerships, creating a paradox where the anxious individual's behaviors inadvertently push their partner away, confirming their worst fears.

Behavioral Patterns and Emotional Responses

The behavioral patterns and emotional responses associated with anxious attachment profoundly influence daily interactions, decision-making, and the overall dynamics of a relationship. Anxious individuals may engage in behaviors such as frequent texting or calling seeking reassurance and may struggle with jealousy or insecurity more intensely than those with other attachment styles.

While intended to protect and preserve the relationship, these behaviors can often lead to conflict and an overwhelming feeling for both partners. Understanding these patterns is crucial for the anxious individual and their partner, as it provides insight into the underlying fears and needs that drive these actions.

Recognizing the signs of anxious attachment within ourselves or our relationships is the first step toward fostering more secure and fulfilling connections. By understanding the emotional, cognitive, and behavioral traits that define this attachment style, we can unravel the complexities of our emotional bonds and work towards healthier, more secure relationships.

In the following sections, we will explore strategies for managing anxious attachment, including developing a more positive self-image, fostering emotional independence, and enhancing communication skills. Together, these tools can help individuals with anxious attachment patterns build the confidence and security necessary for a thriving relationship.

Origins of Anxious Attachment

The Crucial Role of Early Childhood Experiences

The tapestry of human attachment is intricately woven from our earliest interactions with the primary caregivers in our lives. These formative years are not merely stepping stones but are foundational to the emotional architecture that dictates our attachment styles as adults. Early childhood experiences, particularly those involving our bonding experiences with caregivers, are pivotal. Within the crucible of these early interactions, the seeds of anxious attachment are sown or avoided.

Consistent emotional support from caregivers lays the groundwork for secure attachment patterns. When a child feels that their emotional and physical needs are being met with warmth, consistency, and attentiveness, they learn to trust. This trust forms the cornerstone of secure attachment, enabling individuals to approach relationships confidently and openly in adulthood.

Conversely, the lack or inconsistency of such support can lead to the development of anxious attachment styles. Children who experience their caregivers as unpredictably responsive or emotionally unavailable are often left in a state of emotional limbo. The world is unpredictable for these children, and their needs might not always be met, leading to heightened alertness to cues of care and affection.

Impact of Caregiver Responsiveness and Availability

In developing attachment styles, the caregiver's responsiveness and availability role cannot be overstated. A caregiver's ability to sense, interpret, and respond to a child's comfort, security, and autonomy needs is critical. Children who consistently receive responsive care develop a sense of security and self-worth; they believe that they are worthy of love and that others can be relied upon.

However, variations in caregiver availability and emotional presence can lead to the development of anxious attachment patterns. This can manifest in several ways, including over-involvement, where the caregiver is overly attuned to the child's needs, leading to a lack of autonomy and an over-reliance on external validation. On the opposite end of the spectrum is neglect, where a child's emotional or physical needs are frequently ignored, leading to feelings of worthlessness and an insatiable need for closeness and reassurance in adult relationships.

Consider the hypothetical scenario of Emma, a child whose mother was emotionally distant due to her unresolved traumas. Emma learned early on that her emotional expressions were burdensome, leading her to amplify her efforts to gain any form of attention or affection. As an adult, Emma finds herself in a pattern of anxious attachment, constantly seeking reassurance from her partners, mirroring her childhood strategy for gaining her mother's fleeting attention.

Role of Trauma

Traumatic experiences, particularly those occurring in childhood, can significantly exacerbate the development of anxious attachment traits. Trauma can disrupt the child's sense of security and trust in the world, making the fear of abandonment and loss even more pronounced. Whether it's a result of loss, abuse, or neglect, trauma can intensify the need for closeness and reassurance from caregivers or partners, reinforcing the patterns of anxious attachment.

Towards Transformation and Healing

Understanding the origins of anxious attachment is not about assigning blame but about unlocking the door to transformation and healing. Recognizing the profound impact of early childhood experiences and caregiver availability allows individuals to explore the roots of their fears and anxieties within relationships. This understanding is a vital step toward developing secure attachment patterns.

The journey from anxious attachment towards security is not merely possible; it is a path paved with the insights gained from understanding our earliest experiences of love and care. By compassionately examining the past, individuals can reframe their narrative, learning they are worthy of consistent, reliable love and affection. This reevaluation is the first step towards healing, leading to relationships marked by confidence, security, and mutual respect.

Anxious Attachment in Adult Relationships

Manifestations of Anxious Attachment

Anxious attachment profoundly affects adult relationships, manifesting through excessive neediness, fear of abandonment, and challenges in trusting partners. These behaviors often result from deep-seated fears of rejection and a strong desire for closeness and reassurance, leading to emotional intensity and volatility in relationships. Anxiously attached individuals might find themselves constantly seeking validation, worrying excessively about their partner's commitment, and feeling insecure without clear, constant affirmation of love.

Common Challenges

Individuals with anxious attachment face numerous challenges in navigating adult relationships. These challenges include:

- ***Maintaining Independence vs. Closeness:*** Struggling to balance the need for closeness with the desire for independence, leading to conflicts and misunderstandings.
- ***Managing Insecurities:*** The constant battle with insecurities and fears of abandonment can overshadow relationship dynamics, leading to cycles of reassurance seeking and relationship testing.
- ***Effective Communication:*** Difficulty openly and effectively communicating needs without fear of rejection or causing conflict.

Relationship Sabotage

A common challenge for those with anxious attachment is the inadvertent sabotage of relationships. This can occur through behaviors driven by the need for reassurance and fear of abandonment, such as clinging, excessive texting or calling, and seeking constant validation. Though stemming from a place of vulnerability and desire for connection, these actions can overwhelm partners, friends, or colleagues, leading to the very rejection or abandonment the anxious individual fears.

Communication Breakdowns

Effective communication is often a casualty of anxious attachment. The intense emotions and fears experienced by those with anxious attachments can lead to communication breakdowns, particularly during conflict. Instead of expressing needs and desires clearly and constructively, the anxious individual may resort to criticism, accusations, or passive-aggressive behavior driven by their underlying fear of abandonment. This can prevent the resolution of conflicts and exacerbate misunderstandings.

Relationship Dynamics

The dynamics in relationships where one or both partners exhibit anxious attachment styles are characterized by cycles of high dependency and high anxiety. These cycles often include intense periods of closeness followed by fear-driven behaviors that push for reassurance. Such dynamics can strain relationships, as the anxious partner's actions—from fear of loss or rejection—may overwhelm or push away their partner.

The interplay of anxiously attached individuals with secure or avoidant partners also presents unique challenges. With secure partners, anxiously attached individuals might misinterpret stability and security as disinterest or lack of passion. Conversely, when paired with avoidant partners, their need for closeness can trigger the avoidant's fear of intimacy, leading to a push-pull dynamic that exacerbates the anxious partner's fears.

Building Secure Attachments

Developing healthier, more secure attachment patterns is a journey that begins with self-awareness. Recognizing the signs of anxious attachment in oneself and understanding its origins are crucial first steps. From there, individuals can explore new ways of relating that foster security and trust within themselves and their relationships. This might include setting healthy boundaries, cultivating self-reliance, and practicing clear and compassionate communication.

Role of Therapy and Self-Help

Therapy can be a valuable resource for individuals struggling with anxious attachment, providing a safe space to explore the roots of their attachment style and learn new strategies for relating to others. Cognitive-behavioral therapy (CBT), dialectical behavior therapy (DBT), and attachment-based therapy are among the approaches that can help individuals understand and shift their attachment patterns. Additionally, self-help strategies, such as mindfulness, self-compassion exercises, and educational resources like this workbook, can complement therapeutic work, empowering individuals to participate actively in their journey toward healthier relationships.

Anxious attachment can present significant challenges in adult relationships, from romantic partnerships to friendships and professional interactions. However, understanding the manifestations of this attachment style and the dynamics it creates is the first step toward change. By addressing relationship sabotage, the anxious-avoidant trap, communication breakdowns, and taking initial steps toward building secure attachments, individuals can navigate the path to healthier, more fulfilling connections. Therapy and self-help resources play crucial roles in this transformation, offering guidance and support as individuals overcome the patterns established in their earliest relationships.

Deep Dive: The Science Behind Anxious Attachment

Embarking on a journey toward understanding ourselves and the patterns that govern our relationships is a courageous and enlightening endeavor. Among these patterns, anxious attachment is a poignant force, profoundly shaping our interactions and emotional lives. It's a style that, left unexamined, can lead to cycles of distress and dissatisfaction in relationships. However, when we turn the lens of science upon anxious attachment, we uncover knowledge that can transform our experience from confusion and helplessness to empowerment and growth.

For many, the emotional turbulence felt in the throes of anxious attachment can seem mysterious, overwhelming, and beyond control. Yet, there is profound empowerment in demystifying these emotional experiences. Understanding the neurological and psychological underpinnings of anxious attachment does more than illuminate the roots of our behaviors; it provides a map for navigating our way toward healthier, more secure ways of connecting with others.

This deep dive aims to bridge the gap between scientific research and your journey toward secure attachment. By exploring the neurological circuits that light up in moments of anxiety and the psychological theories that explain why we react the way we do, we aim to offer a comprehensive framework for understanding anxious attachment. This is not just about academic knowledge; it's about applying this understanding to foster personal growth and healthier relationships.

As we move forward, remember that this exploration is about identifying what holds us back and recognizing the incredible potential for change within us. The journey from anxious to secure attachment is not a path we walk overnight. Still, with each step forward, armed with knowledge and self-compassion, we move closer to a life of deeper connections and emotional freedom.

Neurological Perspectives on Attachment

Understanding the neurobiological underpinnings of attachment can provide invaluable insights into why we feel and behave the way we do in relationships. Two key brain areas are pivotal in shaping our attachment behaviors: the amygdala and the prefrontal cortex. These regions are instrumental in processing and regulating emotions, and their functionality can greatly influence how we navigate the complex landscape of human connections.

The Amygdala: The Emotional Sentinel

The amygdala, often called the brain's emotional sentinel, plays a crucial role in our survival by processing emotions such as fear and love. It helps us respond to threats and rewards in our environment, a function that extends into social relationships. In the context of attachment, the amygdala is particularly attuned to cues of emotional availability and responsiveness from our partners.

For individuals with anxious attachment, the amygdala can be hyper-responsive to perceived threats of abandonment or rejection. This heightened sensitivity can lead to an amplified emotional response to even subtle cues of disconnection, resulting in the intense anxiety and fear that characterize this attachment style. The amygdala's overactivation in such contexts underscores the emotional volatility experienced by those with anxious attachments, driving the persistent need for reassurance and closeness.

The Prefrontal Cortex: The Emotional Regulator

In contrast to the amygdala's role in emotional processing, the prefrontal cortex regulates these emotions, particularly those deemed excessive or inappropriate. It helps us think before we act, providing a brake on the impulsive responses triggered by the amygdala. This regulatory function is crucial for maintaining emotional balance and engaging in healthy, adaptive relationship behaviors.

However, in individuals with anxious attachment, there can be a discrepancy in the functional balance between the amygdala and the prefrontal cortex. This imbalance often results in a diminished capacity to regulate emotional responses effectively. When the prefrontal cortex is not able to adequately modulate the heightened activity of the amygdala, it can lead to the overwhelming anxiety, fear, and reactive behaviors typical of anxious attachment. The individual may struggle to manage their emotional responses to relationship dynamics, leading to behavior patterns that can strain or sabotage connections.

Functionality Differences in Anxious Attachment

The amygdala and the prefrontal cortex interplay is central to understanding the neurological underpinnings of anxious attachment. The hyperactivation of the amygdala, coupled with the under-regulation by the prefrontal cortex, paints a picture of the neurological landscape that gives rise to the emotional turbulence experienced by those with anxious attachment. This neurobiological perspective helps explain the intensity and volatility of emotions in anxious attachment and highlights potential pathways for therapeutic intervention.

By fostering strategies that enhance the regulatory capacity of the prefrontal cortex, individuals with anxious attachment can learn to modulate their emotional responses more effectively. This can involve practices that increase mindfulness, emotional regulation skills, and cognitive restructuring techniques, all aimed at rebalancing the dynamic between these critical brain regions. Understanding these neurological perspectives empowers individuals with anxious attachment to navigate their emotional world with greater awareness and control, paving the way toward healthier and more secure relationships.

Practical Implications: Navigating Emotional Regulation

Understanding the neurological underpinnings of anxious attachment sets the stage for implementing practical strategies to soothe the amygdala's reactivity and enhance the prefrontal cortex's regulatory capacity. These strategies offer concrete steps individuals can take to manage their emotional responses, fostering healthier relationship dynamics effectively. Below are practical implications and strategies designed to address the emotional regulation challenges associated with anxious attachment.

Soothing the Amygdala's Reactivity

The amygdala's heightened sensitivity in individuals with anxious attachment can lead to overwhelming emotions in response to perceived relationship threats. To soothe the amygdala's reactivity:

Deep Breathing: Engaging in deep, diaphragmatic breathing can activate the body's relaxation response, counteracting the stress response triggered by the amygdala. By focusing on slow, controlled breaths, individuals can help calm their emotional arousal, creating a sense of stability and safety.

Mindfulness and Meditation: Mindfulness practices, including meditation, can help individuals become more aware of their emotional states without becoming entangled in them. This awareness creates a space between the stimulus (perceived threat) and response, reducing the amygdala's reactivity and allowing for more measured reactions to relationship dynamics.

Strengthening the Prefrontal Cortex's Regulatory Capacity

Enhancing the prefrontal cortex's ability to regulate emotional responses is crucial for individuals with anxious attachment. This can be achieved through:

Journaling: Writing about one's thoughts and feelings can help process emotions in a healthy, reflective manner. Journaling can facilitate cognitive restructuring, enabling individuals to challenge and reframe negative thoughts that fuel anxiety and insecurity in relationships.

Cognitive Restructuring: This cognitive-behavioral therapy technique involves identifying and challenging irrational or maladaptive thoughts. By examining the evidence for and against these thoughts, individuals can adopt more balanced and realistic perspectives, strengthening the prefrontal cortex's role in emotional regulation.

Integrating Strategies into Daily Life

Implementing these strategies requires consistency and practice. It's helpful to start small, incorporating techniques like deep breathing or mindfulness into daily routines. Over time, these practices can become more automatic, providing a solid foundation for emotional regulation. Regular journaling or cognitive exercises can reinforce the prefrontal cortex's capacity to modulate emotional responses, leading to more secure and stable relationship patterns.

Seeking Professional Support

While self-help strategies are valuable, working with a therapist can enhance emotional regulation skills. A therapist can offer personalized guidance on implementing these strategies effectively and provide support in navigating the complexities of anxious attachment. Therapeutic approaches, such as cognitive-behavioral, mindfulness-based, and attachment-focused therapy, can be particularly beneficial in addressing the root causes of anxious attachment and fostering healthier ways of relating.

Psychological Perspectives on Attachment

The intricate dance of human relationships is choreographed by a complex interplay of psychological forces, among which attachment theory plays a leading role. This theory, rooted in the work of John Bowlby and Mary Ainsworth, provides a lens through which we can understand how early life experiences sculpt our expectations of ourselves and others, forming mental scripts that guide our interactions and emotional connections. For those grappling with anxious attachment, these scripts often contain themes of unworthiness and doubts about the reliability of others, significantly influencing relationship dynamics.

Attachment Theory and Mental Scripts

Our early interactions with primary caregivers lay the groundwork for mental scripts that shape our perceptions of self-worth and the dependability of those around us. These scripts are powerful narratives that dictate our relationship expectations, influencing how we interpret others' actions and responses. For individuals with an anxious attachment style, these mental scripts may be imbued with fear of abandonment and a deep-seated belief that they must constantly earn love and attention to avoid being left alone.

These scripts are not just passive stories; they shape our reality, driving behaviors that align with the expectation of rejection or disapproval. The anxious individual, governed by a script that highlights their perceived unworthiness, may engage in clinginess, need for reassurance, and hypersensitivity to partners' moods and actions, all in an attempt to secure a love they fear is always on the brink of withdrawal.

Changing the Script

Recognizing and rewriting these negative mental scripts is a formidable yet essential task for those looking to overcome the constraints of anxious attachment. Cognitive-behavioral techniques offer a robust toolkit for this transformative process, enabling individuals to identify, challenge, and revise the detrimental beliefs that underpin their attachment anxieties.

Identifying Negative Beliefs: The first step involves bringing these often-unconscious scripts into the light of awareness. Exercises such as journaling or reflective meditation can help individuals pinpoint the beliefs about self-worth and relational reliability that fuel their anxieties.

Challenging the Script: Once identified, these beliefs must be rigorously questioned. This involves examining the evidence for and against each belief, identifying cognitive distortions, and considering alternative, more balanced perspectives. Questions like "Is this belief always true?" or "What evidence do I have that contradicts this belief?" can be instrumental in this phase.

Rewriting the Narrative: With the old script deconstructed, writing a new narrative begins. This involves crafting affirmations or counter-statements that reflect a healthier self-view and a more secure relationship outlook. For example, I transformed the belief "I am unworthy of love unless I am perfect" to "I am deserving of love, just as I am."

Exercises for Changing the Script

To facilitate the rewriting of these mental scripts, the following exercises can be particularly effective:

Cognitive Restructuring Logs: Keep a daily log of negative thoughts related to attachment and relationships. For each thought, write down a counter-thought or evidence that challenges this negative belief.

Role-Playing: Engage in role-playing exercises, either with a therapist or a trusted friend, to practice responding to situations in ways that reflect your new, healthier scripts.

Visualization Techniques: Visualize scenarios where you act according to your new beliefs about self-worth and relational security. This can help consolidate these beliefs into your mental script.

Changing the deeply ingrained scripts that underlie anxious attachment is both challenging and profoundly rewarding. By applying cognitive-behavioral techniques to identify, challenge, and rewrite negative beliefs, individuals can begin to alter the psychological patterns that have long governed their relationships. This process fosters a more secure attachment style and empowers individuals to engage in relationships with confidence, resilience, and a deep-seated sense of self-worth.

Fear and Insecurity in Anxious Attachment

Fear and insecurity are central to the experience of anxious attachment, casting long shadows over relationships and self-perception. Understanding and managing these fears is crucial for those seeking to navigate anxious attachment more effectively and move towards a sense of security and confidence in their connections with others.

Understanding the Role of Fear

The fear of abandonment and rejection is not unique to individuals with anxious attachment, but it is significantly amplified in their experience. These fears are deeply rooted in early life experiences where the reliability and consistency of emotional support were uncertain. For someone with anxious attachment, these early experiences create a worldview where relationships are seen as precarious, and love is something that must be continuously earned, or it will be withdrawn.

This perspective leads to a heightened vigilance for any signs of disconnection or disapproval from others, interpreting them as precursors to abandonment. The psychological roots of these fears lie in the basic human need for connection and the deeply ingrained belief that one's worthiness of love is conditional and easily forfeited.

Managing Fear Practically

Recognizing and managing fear-based reactions are key to developing healthier, more secure attachments. Several strategies can be effective in addressing the immediate sensations of fear and the underlying beliefs that fuel them:

Grounding Exercises: Techniques such as deep breathing, mindfulness, and sensory grounding (e.g., focusing on the feel of a fabric, the scent of a fragrance, the sound of music) can help calm the physiological arousal associated with fear, bringing the individual back to the present moment and away from catastrophic predictions of their relationships.

Reality Testing: This cognitive strategy involves questioning the evidence for and against one's fears. By examining the factual basis of fears about abandonment or rejection, individuals can begin to differentiate between realistic concerns and those amplified by anxious attachment. Questions like "What evidence do I have that this person will abandon me?" or "Are there alternative explanations for their behavior?" can help in this process.

Expressive Outlets: Engaging in journaling, art, or other forms of creative expression can provide a safe and constructive way to process fear and insecurity. These activities offer an outlet for exploring and expressing emotions, which can be particularly helpful when fears feel overwhelming or difficult to articulate.

Implementing Strategies for Fear Management

Implementing these strategies requires patience and practice, as changing deep-seated emotional responses is gradual. It can be helpful to start by identifying and integrating one or two techniques that resonate with you into your daily routine. Over time, as these practices become more familiar, they can be more readily accessed during moments of heightened fear or insecurity.

Additionally, seeking support from a therapist or joining a support group can provide valuable guidance and encouragement as you work to manage fears related to anxious attachment. These supportive environments can offer insights, validation, and coping strategies, further empowering you to navigate your fears with greater confidence and resilience.

Understanding and managing the fear and insecurity inherent in anxious attachment are vital steps toward forming more secure and fulfilling relationships. By exploring the psychological roots of these fears and implementing practical strategies for managing them, individuals can begin to mitigate the impact of anxious attachment on their lives. This journey toward security may be challenging, but it is also filled with opportunities for growth, self-discovery, and deeper, more meaningful connections with others.

Making the Science Actionable

Transforming the rich tapestry of scientific insight into practical, actionable steps can empower individuals to navigate the complexities of anxious attachment with greater awareness and control. This section introduces self-assessment tools and exercises designed to bridge the gap between understanding and action, enabling readers to apply the science of anxious attachment to their journey toward healthier relationships.

Self-Assessment Tools

Self-assessment is a critical first step in making the science of anxious attachment actionable. By reflecting on how the discussed neurological and psychological aspects manifest in your own life, you can begin to identify patterns and areas for growth. The following tools are designed to facilitate this process:

Anxious Attachment Questionnaire: A series of questions focused on your reactions to relationship stressors, reassurance needs, and abandonment fears. This tool can help clarify the presence and extent of anxious attachment traits in your relationships.

Reflective Prompts: These prompts encourage deeper introspection about your emotional responses and thought patterns. Examples include, "Reflect on a time when you felt abandoned or rejected. What thoughts and feelings arose? How did you react?" and "Consider how you seek reassurance in relationships. What behaviors do you engage in, and what fears are driving those behaviors?"

With a clearer understanding of your attachment style and the behaviors it entails, you can engage in practices designed to address these patterns. The following exercises leverage mindfulness and cognitive techniques to soothe the nervous system and challenge insecure attachment scripts:

Mindfulness Practices for Calming the Nervous System:

Focused Breathing: Sit quietly and focus your attention on your breath. Inhale slowly and deeply through your nose, then exhale gently through your mouth. This practice can help reduce the physiological arousal associated with anxiety.

Body Scan Meditation: Start at your toes and work your way up through your body, noticing any areas of tension without judgment. This technique promotes present-moment awareness and can help interrupt patterns of worry or rumination.

Cognitive Exercises to Challenge Insecure Attachment Scripts:

Thought Record Sheet: Use this tool to track situations that trigger anxious attachment responses, noting the thoughts, emotions, and behaviors that follow. Identifying these patterns is the first step in challenging and changing them.

Reframing Negative Beliefs: Take a belief that contributes to your anxious attachment, such as "I'm not worthy of love," and practice reframing it in a more positive and realistic light, such as "I am worthy of love and capable of forming healthy relationships."

Implementing the Tools and Exercises

Integrating these self-assessment tools and exercises into your daily routine can help make the science of anxious attachment more than just theoretical knowledge. Consistent practice is key to fostering change. You may find it helpful to dedicate a specific time each day to these practices, perhaps incorporating them into your morning routine or using them as a reflective exercise in the evening.

By making the science of anxious attachment actionable through self-assessment tools and tailored exercises, individuals can move beyond understanding their patterns to actively transforming them. This reflection, practice, and growth process opens the door to more secure, fulfilling relationships grounded in self-awareness and emotional resilience. Empowerment lies in applying knowledge, and with these tools at your disposal, you're well-equipped to navigate the path ahead with confidence and clarity.

Impact on Personal and Professional Life

Effects on Personal Development and Self-Esteem

Anxious attachment can significantly hinder personal growth by fostering a dependency that limits self-exploration and autonomy. This dependency often stems from a deep-seated fear of abandonment, leading individuals to seek constant reassurance from others, thus inhibiting their ability to trust in their capabilities and to venture into new experiences independently.

Dependency and Self-Exploration: The need for continuous validation from others can deter individuals from pursuing their interests and desires, restricting personal exploration and self-discovery.

Self-Esteem: Anxious attachment often correlates with feelings of inadequacy, where individuals perceive themselves as not being enough unless affirmed by others. This perception can lead to a heightened sensitivity to rejection, where every critique or failure is internalized as a reflection of their worth.

Consequences for Professional Interactions and Career Development

In the workplace, individuals with an anxious attachment may encounter several challenges that can affect their professional relationships and opportunities for advancement.

Difficulty with Feedback: Fear of criticism can make receiving feedback distressing, often perceived as a personal attack rather than constructive criticism meant for growth.

Fear of Failure: The dread of disappointing others or not meeting expectations can lead to a fear of taking risks or assuming leadership roles, limiting professional development and opportunities for advancement.

Strained Coworker Relationships: Anxious attachment can result in seeking excessive reassurance from colleagues, which may strain professional relationships and teamwork dynamics.

Practical Insights for Mitigation

Self-Reflection: Engage in self-reflection exercises to understand how anxious attachment manifests in your personal and professional life. Recognizing these patterns is the first step toward change.

Seek Feedback Actively: Approach feedback as an opportunity for growth—practice asking for specific examples and suggestions for improvement to reframe your perception of criticism.

Risk-Taking in Small Steps: Gradually expose yourself to new challenges and responsibilities at work. Small victories can build your confidence and reduce the fear of failure.

Addressing the impacts of anxious attachment is crucial for enhancing relationship quality and fostering personal well-being and professional success. By understanding and mitigating the effects of anxious attachment, individuals can develop a more secure attachment style, leading to improved self-esteem, healthier relationships, and career advancement. This workbook aims to provide you with the strategies and insights necessary to embark on this transformative journey, encouraging you to apply the principles within to cultivate a sense of security and confidence in all aspects of life.

Chapter Exercises

Anxious Attachment Self-Assessment Quiz

This quiz is designed to help you reflect on your relationship behaviors and feelings. Rate how much you agree with each statement using the following scale:

1. Strongly Disagree
2. Disagree
3. Neutral
4. Agree
5. Strongly Agree

Record your answers to gain insight into your attachment style.

1. I often worry that my partner doesn't love me as much as I love them.
2. I find myself constantly needing reassurance from my partner that they are committed to me.
3. The thought of my partner leaving me makes me very anxious or panicky.
4. I tend to be very sensitive to changes in my partner's mood or behavior, worrying they might lose interest in me.
5. I frequently check my partner's social media or texts to feel reassured about our relationship.
6. I often sacrifice my needs to please my partner, fearing they might drift away.
7. The idea of being alone or single makes me feel uncomfortable or anxious.
8. I sometimes feel like I'm too emotionally dependent on my partner, but I can't help it.
9. When I sense my partner is pulling away, even slightly, I tend to react strongly, either by clinging tighter or getting upset.
10. I frequently replay my partner's words or actions, worried I might have missed signs of dissatisfaction with our relationship.
11. I often need more affection and intimacy from my partner than they seem willing to give.
12. I fear my partner will lose interest in me if I don't constantly try.
13. I get anxious when my partner spends time with others and I'm not included.

14. I have difficulty focusing on other areas of my life when worrying about my relationship.
15. I tend to take my partner's mood or casual remarks personally.
16. I worry about being too much for my partner and that they might find someone better.
17. I struggle with feeling that my partner's reassurance never quite satisfies my need for security.
18. I sometimes act out or make impulsive decisions to get my partner's attention.
19. I have difficulty trusting my partner's words if their actions don't always match.
20. The state of my relationship heavily influences my mood and happiness.

Scoring Guide for the Anxious Attachment Self-Assessment Quiz

After completing the quiz, total your score by adding the numbers from your responses. Each statement is rated on a scale from 1 to 5, where 1 = Strongly Disagree and 5 = Strongly Agree. The sum of your scores will help indicate your tendency toward anxious attachment in relationships.

Score Interpretation:

- **20-40: Low Tendency Towards Anxious Attachment.** You may have moments of concern in your relationships, but they do not frequently impact your sense of security or well-being. You generally feel confident and secure in your attachments.

- **41-60: Moderate Tendency Towards Anxious Attachment.** You might often feel anxious about your relationships and seek reassurance more than you'd like. While not always overwhelming, these feelings may sometimes challenge your sense of security and relationship satisfaction.

- **61-80: High Tendency Towards Anxious Attachment.** You frequently experience significant anxiety in your relationships, often seeking reassurance and fearing abandonment. These feelings may significantly impact your relationship satisfaction and sense of security.

- **81-100: Very High Tendency Towards Anxious Attachment.** Your responses indicate a strong presence of anxious attachment traits. You likely experience constant worry about your relationships, seeking reassurance, and fearing abandonment, which may often interfere with your relationship dynamics and personal well-being.

Remember, this quiz is a tool for self-reflection and not a diagnostic assessment. High scores indicating a tendency towards anxious attachment can be a starting point for further exploration and understanding of your attachment style. If you recognize patterns that negatively impact your life or relationships, consider consulting a mental health professional for support and guidance.

Journaling Prompts on Attachment History

Journaling about one's attachment history can uncover insights into how early relationships and experiences have shaped current attachment styles. These prompts are designed to explore those foundational experiences, aiding in understanding and possibly transforming your relationship approach.

- Describe Your Earliest Memory of Feeling Safe and Loved: Reflect on who was with you, what was happening, and how it made you feel.

- Recall a Time You Felt Abandoned or Alone as a Child: Who was involved? What happened, and how did you cope with those feelings then?

- Think About Your Primary Caregivers' Approach to Comfort and Affection: Were they readily available and responsive to your needs? How did their style of showing love or comfort affect your sense of security?

- Identify Significant Losses or Changes in Your Early Life: How did these events impact your feelings about trust and security in relationships?

- Consider the Emotional Climate of Your Childhood Home: Was it open and expressive, or more reserved and distant? How has this shaped your emotional expression and needs in relationships?

- Reflect on Your Experiences with Peers During Early School Years: Were you able to form secure friendships, or did you often feel left out or misunderstood? How have these experiences influenced your social interactions as an adult?

- Analyze Your First Romantic Relationship: How did your behaviors and feelings in this relationship mirror those in your relationships with caregivers or peers?

- Think About Patterns in Your Adult Relationships: Can you identify recurring themes, behaviors, or types of partners that echo your early attachment experiences?

- Contemplate Any Moments of Realization About Your Attachment Style: Have there been pivotal moments or relationships that made you aware of your anxious attachment tendencies?

- Envision the Type of Attachment You Desire: What steps can you take to move toward a more secure attachment style based on your reflections?

Instructions for Journaling

Choose a Quiet Time and Space: Ensure you have privacy and won't be interrupted. This is your time to reflect and explore your thoughts and feelings.

Write Freely: Don't worry about grammar or style. The goal is to express your thoughts and feelings as openly and honestly as possible.

Be Patient with Yourself: Some of these prompts may evoke strong emotions. Take breaks if you need to, and consider seeking support from a therapist if you find certain areas particularly challenging to explore.

Regular Reflection: Consider revisiting these prompts periodically. Your insights and feelings may evolve as you grow and change.

Trigger Mapping Exercise Guide

Objective:

To identify common and personal triggers that activate anxious attachment responses, allowing for deeper self-awareness and the development of healthier coping strategies.

Materials Needed:

A journal or digital document for recording reflections, a quiet space for introspection.

Step 1: List Common Triggers for Anxious Attachment

Partner's Delayed Responses: Worrying when a partner does not quickly reply to texts or calls.

Changes in Routine or Plans: Feeling anxious when unexpected changes occur in your partner's schedule or plans.

Social Media Activity: Overanalyzing a partner's interactions on social media platforms.

Perceived Emotional Withdrawal: Sensing a partner is less emotionally available or distant.

Conflicts or Disagreements: Worrying that disagreements will lead to abandonment.

Expressions of Independence by Partner: Feeling threatened when a partner seeks time alone or pursues personal interests.

Signs of Dissatisfaction: Interpreting minor criticisms or feedback as signs of a partner's waning interest.

Step 2: Reflect on Personal Triggers

After listing common triggers, reflect on your triggers. Consider situations in past or current relationships where you felt particularly anxious or insecure. Write down these instances.

Step 3: Analyze Each Trigger

For each identified trigger, analyze why it makes you feel anxious, the thoughts or beliefs activated, and how you typically respond and envision a healthier response.

Step 4: Develop Coping Strategies

Based on your reflections, brainstorm coping strategies for each trigger, including self-soothing techniques, rational responses, or communication needs effectively.

Step 5: Implementation Plan

Create an action plan for implementing these coping strategies, deciding on specific steps, reminders, and support.

Conclusion

The Trigger Mapping Exercise is a dynamic process. Regularly revisiting and updating your trigger map can be valuable to your journey toward secure attachment and emotional resilience.

Sharing and Feedback

Consider sharing your insights from this exercise with a trusted friend, family member, or therapist for additional perspectives and support.

Emotional Response Diary Guide

Purpose:

The diary aims to increase self-awareness regarding anxious attachment behaviors and the emotions they evoke. Tracking these experiences daily can illuminate patterns and triggers, fostering a deeper understanding of one's attachment style and promoting healthier emotional regulation.

Format:

The diary can be maintained in a digital document, a dedicated notebook, or any format that is convenient and regularly accessible.

Daily Entries Should Include:

1. **Date and Time:** Note the date and time of the anxious attachment behavior or feeling.
2. **Situation:** Describe the situation or interaction that preceded or triggered the anxious response. Include as many details as necessary.

3. ***Emotions:*** Record the emotions felt during the situation using specific descriptors and rate the intensity on a scale of 1 to 10.
4. ***Physical Sensations:*** Note any physical sensations experienced. This helps connect emotional states with physical responses.
5. ***Thoughts:*** Write down the thoughts or beliefs that went through your mind.
6. ***Behavior:*** Detail your response and emotions resulting from the situation.
7. ***Self-Soothing Techniques Used:*** Note any coping or self-soothing techniques and rate their effectiveness.
8. ***Reflection:*** After some time, reflect on the situation, considering alternative interpretations and healthier coping mechanisms.

Weekly Review:

Review your entries at the end of each week to identify patterns, common triggers, and which coping strategies were most effective. This review can offer valuable insights into your emotional triggers and progress in managing anxious attachment behaviors.

How to Use This Diary for Growth:

- ***Identify Patterns:*** Look for recurring situations, thoughts, or emotions that trigger anxious attachment behaviors.
- ***Understand Triggers:*** Recognizing triggers can empower you to prepare or respond more healthily in future situations.
- ***Evaluate Coping Strategies:*** Determine which coping mechanisms are effective and which are not.

Identifying Needs and Desires in Relationships

The following exercises help individuals distinguish between genuine needs and desires in their relationships and those driven by anxious attachment or anxiety. By clarifying these aspects, individuals can approach their relationships more healthily and authentically.

Exercise 1: Distinguishing Needs from Anxieties

Objective: To differentiate between what you genuinely need in a relationship for fulfillment and what desires may stem from anxiety.

Instructions:
1. ***List Your Needs and Desires:*** Write down everything you need and desire from a relationship.

2. ***Categorize Each Item:*** Next to each need or desire, categorize it as a 'Genuine Need,' 'Anxiety-Driven,' or 'Uncertain.'

3. ***Reflect on Your Categories:*** Consider why each category is important for your happiness and fulfillment or what fears or insecurities these may be masking.

4. ***Action Plan:*** Focus on how to meet your genuine needs through self-care, communication, and boundary-setting in your relationships.

Exercise 2: Reflecting on Past Relationships

Objective: To analyze past relationships for patterns in your needs and how anxiety influenced your desires and actions.

Instructions:
1. ***Choose Three Past Relationships to Analyze:*** These can be romantic, familial, or friendships.

2. ***Identify Expressed Needs and Desires:*** List your needs and desires for each relationship.

3. ***Evaluate Outcomes:*** Reflect on whether these needs were met and how anxiety-driven desires affected the dynamics.

4. ***Lessons Learned:*** Write down insights gained about your genuine needs versus anxiety-driven desires.

Exercise 3: Visualization for Clarity

Objective: To use visualization to clarify your needs and desires in a relationship free from anxiety's influence.

Instructions:

1. Find a Quiet Space*:* Sit comfortably where you won't be disturbed.

2. Visualize Your Ideal Relationship: Imagine a relationship where you feel secure, loved, and understood.

3. Identify Your Feelings and Needs: Focus on what needs are being met in this visualization.

4. Reflect on the Absence of Anxiety: Consider how the absence of anxiety changes what you seek from the relationship.

Chapter 2
The Role of Emotional Intelligence in Relationships

Introduction to Emotional Intelligence (EQ)

Objective: The beginning of Chapter 2 is dedicated to unfolding the concept of Emotional Intelligence (EQ), a pivotal construct in understanding ourselves and our interactions with others. This section aims to provide readers with a foundational understanding of EQ, tracing its historical development and elucidating its paramount importance in contemporary relationships.

Definition and Overview of EQ:

Emotional Intelligence (EQ) is the capacity to be aware of, control, and express one's emotions and to handle interpersonal relationships judiciously and empathetically. It involves the ability to recognize, understand, manage, and use one's own emotions in positive ways to relieve stress, communicate effectively, empathize with others, overcome challenges, and defuse conflict. EQ also encompasses the skill to recognize and influence the emotions of others, fostering empathy and communication in personal and professional relationships.

At the heart of EQ lies the recognition that emotions are not obstacles to be suppressed or ignored but valuable sources of information that can guide our behaviors and decisions. This awareness extends beyond merely identifying one's emotional states to understanding how emotions can impact others, influence social dynamics, and affect decision-making processes.

The Importance of EQ in Personal Development and Social Interactions:

The significance of EQ in our lives cannot be overstated. In personal development, EQ is a cornerstone for self-awareness, self-regulation, motivation, empathy, and social skills.

These competencies enable individuals to navigate the complexities of emotions, enhancing personal well-being and fostering resilience. EQ skills are crucial for personal growth, as they help individuals understand and manage their emotional experiences, promoting a sense of psychological well-being and self-efficacy.

In the realm of social interactions, EQ is equally vital. It underpins our ability to communicate effectively, build and maintain relationships, empathize with others, and manage social networks. High EQ individuals are adept at reading social cues, understanding others' emotional states, and responding appropriately, which can lead to more satisfying and supportive relationships. In contemporary relationships, where communication and mutual understanding are paramount, EQ enhances intimacy, trust, and connection.

Moreover, in a world increasingly recognizing the value of emotional health and intelligence, EQ is emerging as a critical factor in achieving success and fulfillment in both personal and professional domains. It facilitates conflict resolution, promotes empathy and understanding, and strengthens interpersonal bonds, making it an indispensable asset in the journey toward secure and fulfilling relationships.

In the following sections, we will delve deeper into the components of Emotional Intelligence, exploring how each facet contributes to the dynamics of relationships and providing practical strategies for enhancing EQ in the context of anxious attachment. Through this exploration, readers will gain insights into the transformative power of EQ in transforming relationship fears into confidence and security in life and love.

Relevance of EQ in Contemporary Relationships

In the intricate dance of contemporary relationships, Emotional Intelligence (EQ) plays a pivotal role in shaping how we connect, communicate, and resolve conflicts. As we navigate the complexities of modern social and romantic relationships, the significance of EQ cannot be overstated. This section delves into the essence of EQ in today's interpersonal dynamics, highlighting its impact on communication, empathy, and conflict resolution. It offers insights into how honing these emotional skills can lead to more satisfying and resilient relationships.

Impact on Communication

Effective communication is the bedrock of any healthy relationship, and EQ is its cornerstone. EQ enhances our ability to convey thoughts and feelings clearly, listen attentively, and respond appropriately. It enables us to read between the lines, picking up on non-verbal cues and emotional undercurrents. For instance, a partner with high EQ might notice when their significant other needs support before a word is even spoken, bridging gaps in understanding and fostering a deeper connection.

Enhancing Empathy

Empathy, a core component of EQ, allows us to step into the shoes of others, feel what they feel, and see the world from their perspective. This empathetic connection is crucial in social and romantic relationships, as it builds emotional intimacy and trust. When we empathize, we validate our partner's feelings, making them feel seen, heard, and understood. This mutual understanding paves the way for stronger, more connected relationships.

Conflict Resolution

Conflicts, while inevitable, do not have to lead to breakdowns in relationships. EQ equips us with the tools to navigate disagreements with compassion, patience, and understanding. High EQ individuals approach conflicts as opportunities for growth, seeking win-win solutions that respect both parties' needs and emotions. Through EQ, we learn to manage our reactions, communicate our grievances constructively, and empathize with the other person's viewpoint, transforming potential conflicts into bonding moments.

Enhancing Relationship Satisfaction and Resilience

Developing EQ can significantly enhance relationship satisfaction and resilience. We can avoid misunderstandings and reduce relational stress by managing our emotions effectively. EQ fosters a supportive and nurturing environment where both partners feel empowered to express themselves freely and work together to overcome challenges. Couples with high EQ tend to have more fulfilling and lasting relationships, as they can adapt to changes, support each other through hardships, and celebrate successes together.

As we set the stage to delve deeper into the components of EQ, it's clear that mastering these emotional skills is not just beneficial but essential for fostering healthier, more fulfilling relationships. Whether it's through improving communication, deepening empathy, or navigating conflicts with grace, EQ stands as a beacon guiding us toward more meaningful connections. In the following chapters, we will explore how you can apply these principles to enrich your relationships, offering practical strategies and insights to enhance your emotional intelligence. Prepare to embark on a journey that promises to transform not only how you relate to others but also how you understand yourself.

EQ and Anxious Attachment

Identifying Triggers of Anxious Attachment Through EQ

Emotional Intelligence (EQ) plays a pivotal role in recognizing and understanding the triggers of anxious attachment. By developing self-awareness, a key component of EQ, individuals can become more attuned to the specific situations or behaviors that evoke feelings of insecurity and anxiety in their relationships. This awareness is the first step toward addressing and managing anxious attachment tendencies.

The Interplay Between EQ and Attachment Styles

The relationship between EQ and attachment styles is significant and complex. Individuals with higher levels of emotional intelligence are better equipped to understand and navigate the challenges associated with their attachment styles. Enhancing EQ can lead to more secure relationship patterns for those with an anxious attachment. This improvement comes from the ability to manage one's emotions effectively, understand the emotions of others, and respond to relationship dynamics more adaptively and constructively.

Strategies to Enhance EQ for Managing Anxious Attachment

Enhancing EQ involves developing skills across its various components: self-awareness, self-regulation, motivation, empathy, and social skills. Here are strategies tailored for managing anxious attachment:

Self-Awareness: Engage in regular self-reflection to better understand your emotional triggers and the underlying beliefs that contribute to anxious attachment.

Self-Regulation: Practice mindfulness and deep breathing techniques to manage emotional responses and reduce anxiety in triggering situations.

Motivation: Redirect your focus towards personal growth and developing a sense of purpose independent of your relationships. This can help in reducing dependency on external validation.

Empathy: Cultivate empathy towards yourself and others. Understanding and accepting your emotional needs and your partner's can lead to healthier interactions.

Social Skills: Work on communication and conflict resolution skills to improve interactions and strengthen relationships. This includes practicing active listening, asserting needs, and addressing conflicts constructively.

Emotional intelligence offers valuable tools for individuals with anxious attachments to understand and manage their emotional responses and relationship dynamics more effectively. By identifying triggers, understanding the interplay between EQ and attachment styles, and employing strategies to enhance EQ, individuals can work towards developing more secure attachment patterns in their relationships. This process benefits personal and romantic relationships and improves overall emotional growth and well-being.

Developing EQ to Improve Relationship Dynamics

Emotional Awareness Exercises

Emotional awareness fosters emotional intelligence (EQ) and improves relationship dynamics. Emotional awareness involves recognizing and understanding one's emotions and how they influence interactions with others. Here are some exercises to enhance emotional awareness:

Daily Emotion Tracking: Dedicate a few minutes each day to identify and record your emotions, noting the circumstances that triggered these feelings. This practice helps recognize patterns and emotions' impact on decision-making and relationships.

Emotional Labeling: Work on accurately labeling your emotions. Instead of using broad terms like 'good' or 'bad,' try to specify whether you're feeling frustrated, anxious, excited, or content. This specificity can enhance emotional understanding and communication.

Reflecting on How Emotions Influence Relationship Interactions

Reflection is a powerful tool for understanding how emotions influence relationship dynamics. Consider these practices:

Journaling: Regularly write about significant interactions with others, focusing on how emotions affected the interaction. Reflect on positive and negative experiences to gain insights into your emotional responses and their consequences.

Feedback Seeking: Ask close friends or family members how they perceive your emotional reactions. This external perspective can provide valuable insights into your emotional impact on others.

Enhancing Emotional Clarity

Gaining clarity about one's emotions is crucial for effective emotional regulation and the development of EQ. Techniques to enhance emotional clarity include:

Mindfulness Meditation: Engage in mindfulness meditation focusing on emotions. This practice can help distinguish between surface emotions and the deeper feelings driving them, fostering a deeper understanding of emotional experiences.

Body Scan Exercises: Perform regular body scans to notice any physical sensations associated with emotions. This technique helps recognize emotions' physical manifestations and increases emotional clarity.

Techniques for Distinguishing Between Surface and Underlying Emotions

Understanding the difference between immediate, surface-level emotions and the deeper, underlying ones is essential for emotional intelligence. Techniques include:

Situation Analysis: When experiencing strong emotions, take a step back to analyze the situation. Ask yourself what deeper feelings might be driving your immediate reaction. This can reveal underlying issues or needs.

Emotional Decomposition: Break down complex emotional experiences into their parts. For example, anger might be composed of frustration, hurt, and fear. Identifying these components can provide clearer pathways for addressing and expressing these emotions.

Tools for Understanding Complex Emotional Experiences

Complex emotional experiences require sophisticated tools for understanding. Some effective tools include:

Emotion Wheels: Use emotion wheels, which provide a visual map of how basic emotions can combine to create complex feelings to understand better and articulate your emotional states.

Therapeutic Techniques: Techniques like cognitive behavioral therapy (CBT) can offer strategies for dissecting and understanding complex emotions and provide ways to address and regulate them.

Developing emotional intelligence through awareness and clarity exercises can significantly improve relationship dynamics. By becoming more attuned to your emotional states and their influences on interactions, you can foster deeper connections, navigate conflicts more effectively, and build a foundation for healthy, satisfying relationships.

Chapter Exercises

Empathetic Validation Exercise

Objective:

This exercise is designed to enhance your ability to validate the feelings of others without attempting to solve their problems or change how they feel. Practicing empathetic validation fosters deeper connections and shows genuine understanding and support.

Materials Needed:

- An open and compassionate mindset.
- A partner, friend, or family member willing to share their feelings with you.
- A quiet, comfortable space conducive to open conversation.

Steps to Practice Empathetic Validation:

Step 1: Find a Willing Participant
Choose someone who trusts you enough to share their feelings openly. Explain the purpose of the exercise: to practice listening and validating feelings without offering solutions or judgment.

Step 2: Active Listening
When your chosen participant begins to share, focus entirely on listening. Resist the urge to think about what advice to give or how to respond. Just listen.

Step 3: Reflect Back
Once they have finished sharing, reflect on what you heard to ensure you've understood them correctly.

Use phrases like, "It sounds like you're feeling…" or "So, you're feeling upset because…".

Step 4: Validate Their Feelings

After reflecting on their feelings, validate them. Acknowledge that their feelings are understandable and valid given their situation. You might say, "It makes sense you'd feel that way given what happened," or "Anyone in your situation would feel similarly."

Step 5: Offer Support Without Solutions

Instead of offering solutions, ask how you can support them. Say, "How can I best support you right now?" Remember, the goal is not to fix the problem but to show empathy and understanding.

Examples:

- Situation: Your friend is upset about a misunderstanding with another friend.
- Active Listening: You listen attentively without interrupting.
- Reflect: "You're hurt because Alex misunderstood you, right?
- Validate: "It's completely understandable you'd feel hurt after being misunderstood like that."
- Support: "I'm here for you. Would you like to talk more about it, or is there something else to help you feel supported?"

Reflection:

After the exercise, reflect on the experience in your journal. How did focusing solely on validating feelings without jumping to solutions feel? Did you notice any shift in the emotional atmosphere or the other person's demeanor?

Conclusion:

Empathetic validation is a powerful tool in strengthening relationships and building emotional intimacy. By practicing this exercise, you learn to become a better listener and supporter, creating a safe space for others to express their feelings and feel truly heard and understood.

Letter to Your Future Self-Exercise

Objective

This exercise encourages you to deeply self-reflect and think about your journey toward developing secure attachments in your relationships. It's about articulating your hopes, goals, and commitments to your future emotional and relational well-being.

Materials Needed

- Writing materials (pen and paper) or a digital device for typing
- A quiet, comfortable space for reflection

Introduction

Begin by understanding the purpose of this letter: to express your current thoughts, feelings, and aspirations regarding your attachment style and relationships. Envision a future where you've achieved secure attachment and consider its impact on your relationships and overall well-being.

Reflect on Your Current State

Start your letter by reflecting on your current understanding of your attachment style. Acknowledge your patterns in relationships, your emotional needs, and the challenges you face.

Envision Your Future Self

Imagine your future self with a cultivated secure attachment style. Describe the transformation in your relationship approach, emotional resilience, and effectiveness in navigating conflicts and expressing needs and boundaries.

Outline Your Hopes and Goals

Detail your hopes for your relationships and personal growth. Set goals for emotional regulation, communication, self-esteem, and forming healthy, fulfilling relationships.

Commitments to Your Future Self

Discuss your commitments to achieve these goals, such as therapy, mindfulness practice, or actively working on communication and boundary-setting skills.

Message of Support and Encouragement

End your letter with supportive and encouraging words for your future self. Remind yourself of your strengths, resilience, and capacity for growth and change.

Seal and Date the Letter

Seal your letter in an envelope and mark it with a future date when you plan to open it. This act symbolizes your commitment to growth and is a milestone to look forward to.

Conclusion

This letter is a promise to yourself—a testament to your commitment to growth, healing, and the pursuit of secure attachment in your relationships. It will serve as a motivational and encouraging reminder of your goals and the steps you're prepared to take to achieve them.

Challenging Insecure Thoughts Exercise

What You'll Need:

- A peaceful spot for some introspection.
- A notebook or a digital device to jot down your thoughts.

Your Mission:

Embark on a journey to confront those nagging, insecure thoughts that sometimes cloud your confidence. This exercise is your toolkit for turning those doubts inside out, showcasing the secure, resilient you that's been there all along.

Getting Started:

Step 1: Spotting the Insecurities
Consider recent moments when doubt crept into your mind, especially in your relationships. Maybe it was a whisper telling you you're not enough or a shadow of fear about opening up. Write these thoughts down; these are your starting points.

Step 2: Remember Your Strengths
Now, for each of those shaky thoughts, I want you to recall a time when you stood strong. Maybe you had a heart-to-heart, and it went well, or you set a boundary, and it was respected. These are your proofs of secure behavior—your relationship superpowers.

Step 3: The Transformation
Besides each insecure thought, let's get analytical. Write down how your remembered strength contradicts that doubt. This is where you challenge the insecurity, transforming it with evidence of your capability and resilience.

Step 4: Affirm Your Truth
Convert these new, empowered perspectives into affirmations. Suppose the insecurity was about always feeling left out, and you remembered when you were included and valued. In that case, your affirmation might be, "I am appreciated and belong in my relationships."

Step 5: Repeat and Reinforce
Make these affirmations part of your daily mantra. Say them out loud, write them down each morning, or keep them close on your phone. The more you reinforce these truths, the more they'll become your automatic response to those old insecurities.

Reflection:

After a few weeks, revisit this exercise. How do you feel about those initial insecurities now? Are the affirmations starting to feel like second nature? Remember, growth is a journey, and every step you take towards challenging your insecurities is a step towards a more secure, confident you.

Conclusion:

This exercise isn't just about tackling insecurities; it's about recognizing and celebrating the strength and security you already possess. You're building a foundation of confidence that will support you in all your relationships.

Rejection Processing Exercise

Objective:

This exercise invites you to gently confront and process the feelings surrounding past rejections. By acknowledging and understanding these emotions, you can mitigate their influence on your present and future relationships, allowing for healing and growth.

What You'll Need:

- A quiet space where you can reflect without interruptions.
- A journal or any device where you can comfortably write down your thoughts and feelings.
- Compassion and patience for yourself as you navigate through these reflections.

Your Guide to Healing:

Step 1: Recall and Record

Begin by recalling instances of rejection you've experienced in your life. These might include romantic rejections, friendships that didn't work out, or instances where you felt excluded or undervalued. Write each instance down, focusing on the facts without delving into the emotions.

Step 2: Identify Your Feelings

Next to each instance of rejection, jot down how you felt then. Try to name the emotions as precisely as you can—hurt, betrayed, lonely, inadequate. Recognizing these feelings is the first step toward processing them.

Step 3: Reflect on the Impact
Reflect on how these experiences of rejection have influenced your behavior or feelings in current relationships. Are there patterns of thought or behavior you can trace back to these moments? Write these reflections down as honestly as you can.

Step 4: Seek the Lessons
For each rejection, ask yourself what you learned from the experience. Perhaps you discovered more about your needs in relationships or grew stronger in your sense of self. There's always a silver lining, even if it's just the knowledge that you survived and moved forward.

Step 5: Write a Letter of Forgiveness
Choose one of the instances of rejection that still weighs heavily on you. Please write a letter to the person involved, expressing your feelings and the impact it had on you. Then, write about your decision to forgive them and yourself. You don't have to send this letter—it's a symbolic gesture to help you let go and heal.

Step 6: Create Affirmations
Based on your reflections, create a few positive affirmations to counteract the negative beliefs that stemmed from these rejections. For instance, if you often feel unworthy of love because of past rejections, your affirmation could be, "I am worthy of love and belonging."

Examples:

- Rejection Instance: Being ghosted after a few dates.
- Feelings: Confused, inadequate, abandoned.
- Impact on Current Relationships: Fear of opening up, expecting others to leave suddenly.
- Lesson: Communication is crucial for me in relationships; not everyone's actions reflect my worth.
- Affirmation: "My worth is not defined by others' inability to see it."

Step 7: Practice Self-Compassion
Remember that rejection is a universal experience—it doesn't reflect your worth or desirability as a person or partner. Practice treating yourself with the same kindness and understanding you'd offer a friend.

Conclusion:

Processing past rejections is a crucial step towards healing and building healthier relationships. By confronting these experiences head-on, you empower yourself to move forward with a stronger, more open heart. Remember, each step in this exercise is a step towards self-love and resilience.

Empathy Mapping Exercise

Objective:

Empathy mapping is a powerful exercise designed to deepen your understanding of the people in your life by exploring their perspectives, feelings, and motivations. This tool can enhance your empathy, improving your relationships through greater insight and connection.

Materials Needed:

- A quiet space where you can reflect without distractions.
- A journal or digital device for creating your empathy maps.
- Pens or markers if you prefer to draw or visually map your thoughts.

Steps to Create an Empathy Map:

Step 1: Choose a Person
Start by selecting someone in your life you want to understand better. It could be a partner, friend, family member, or colleague.

Step 2: Draw or Outline Your Map
Divide your page into four sections: **Thinking**, **Feeling**, **Seeing**, and **Hearing**. These sections will help you organize your thoughts as you consider different aspects of this person's experience.

Step 3: Fill in the Map
- *Thinking:* What might this person think about in situations involving you or their daily life? What concerns or goals occupy their mind?

- *Feeling:* Identify how this person feels within your shared interactions or in their own experiences. Are there emotions they show openly or perhaps hide?
- *Seeing:* Consider what this person sees in their environment, interactions with others, and relationships with you. How might their physical or social surroundings influence their perspective?
- *Hearing:* Reflect on what this person hears from you, others, and the world around them. What messages or feedback are they receiving, and how might this affect their views or feelings?

Step 4: Reflect on Insights

After completing your empathy map, take some time to reflect on what insights you've gained. How does seeing the world from their perspective change your understanding of their actions or reactions?

Step 5: Apply Your Insights

Think about how you can use these insights to improve your interactions with this person. Consider adjustments in your communication, actions, or support to better align with their needs and perspectives.

Example:

Person: My partner

- *Thinking:* "I have so much work to do. I hope we can spend some quality time together this weekend."
- *Feeling:* They might be depressed from work.
- *Seeing:* They see me busy with my hobbies and might think I don't want to spend time with them.
- *Hearing:* They've heard me say, "We'll do something fun this weekend," which might reassure them.

Insights: I realize they might feel neglected when absorbed in my activities. They value our shared time and need reassurance about our plans.

Action: I'll consciously express my excitement about our weekend plans and check in during the week to see how they feel.

Conclusion:

Empathy mapping is a dynamic way to foster understanding and compassion in your relationships. Seeing the world from someone else's viewpoint opens the door to deeper connections and more meaningful interactions. This exercise encourages empathy and adaptability, key components of strong, healthy relationships.

Chapter 3
Identifying Anxious Behaviors in Relationships

This chapter provides an overview of anxious attachment behaviors in relationships and emphasizes the significance of recognizing these behaviors for personal growth and relationship improvement. Understanding and identifying anxious behaviors is crucial for developing strategies to manage them effectively, fostering healthier and more secure relationships.

Overview of Anxious Attachment Behaviors in Relationships

Anxious attachment behaviors often manifest as a need for constant reassurance, hypersensitivity to a partner's actions and moods, fear of abandonment and rejection, clinging and needy behavior, difficulty trusting partners, and overanalyzing relationship dynamics. Recognizing these behaviors is the first step in addressing anxious attachment and working towards more secure attachment patterns.

The Significance of Recognizing These Behaviors

Identifying anxious attachment behaviors is vital for several reasons. It allows individuals to gain insights into their attachment style and understand how it affects their relationships. This awareness enables individuals to work on their emotional responses and develop healthier ways of relating to others. Recognizing and addressing anxious behaviors can lead to significant personal growth and improved relationship dynamics.

Individuals can embark on a journey of personal transformation by identifying and understanding anxious attachment behaviors. Recognizing these behaviors and their impact, one **can develop strategies to manage anxiety, enhance emotional intelligence,** and foster secure and satisfying relationships. This chapter sets the foundation for exploring techniques and exercises to address anxious attachment behaviors in subsequent sections.

Common Behaviors and Patterns Associated with Anxious Attachment

Seeking Constant Reassurance

One of the hallmark behaviors of anxious attachment is the seeking of constant reassurance. Individuals with an anxious attachment style often require ongoing validation from their partners to feel secure in the relationship. This need for reassurance stems from deep-seated fears of abandonment and a worry that they are not enough for their partners.

The impact of this behavior on relationships can be significant. On the one hand, it can strain the partner considerably, who may feel overwhelmed by the constant need to provide assurance. On the other hand, the individual seeking reassurance might never fully experience a sense of security, as external validation can only temporarily relieve their underlying anxieties.

Understanding this need for validation is crucial for both partners. For the individual with anxious attachment, recognizing this pattern is the first step towards developing healthier ways of seeking and experiencing reassurance. It involves cultivating self-esteem and learning to internalize a sense of worth that is not solely dependent on their partner's affirmations.

For their partners, understanding can lead to compassion and a more supportive approach to addressing these needs. It's about finding a balance between providing reassurance and encouraging the development of self-soothing and independence.

In essence, the need for constant reassurance in anxious attachment reflects deeper issues related to self-worth and fear of loss. Addressing these issues directly through communication, therapy, and personal development can mitigate the impact on the relationship and promote a more secure attachment style.

Hypersensitivity to Partner's Actions and Moods

Hypersensitivity to a partner's actions and moods is a common characteristic of individuals with anxious attachment. This hypersensitivity often results from a heightened perception of potential threats to the relationship's stability. Individuals may read into their partner's moods or actions more deeply than intended, seeing them as signs of diminishing affection or interest. This perception significantly influences their reactions, leading to behaviors aimed at seeking reassurance or attempting to avoid perceived abandonment.

Fear of Abandonment and Rejection

The fear of abandonment and rejection is at the core of anxious attachment behaviors. This fear can prompt individuals to remain in a constant state of alertness to any signs that their partner might leave them, whether there is a real risk or not. Identifying these underlying fears is crucial for addressing anxious attachment behaviors. Acknowledging and confronting these fears can help individuals understand their reactions and work towards more secure attachment patterns.

Clinging and Needy Behavior

Clinging and needy behavior, while often stemming from a desire for closeness and connection, can strain relationships when it crosses into anxious dependency. Distinguishing between healthy closeness and anxious dependency involves recognizing when the desire for proximity is driven by fear and insecurity rather than mutual affection and connection. Healthy closeness is characterized by mutual respect for independence and individuality, whereas anxious dependency often disregards personal boundaries and the partner's need for space. Understanding this distinction is essential for developing healthier attachment behaviors and fostering a more balanced and fulfilling relationship.

Difficulty Trusting Partners

Difficulty trusting partners is a common issue for those with anxious attachment styles. This challenge often stems from past experiences of betrayal or inconsistency, leading to a protective mechanism that errs on the side of caution. Trust issues rooted in anxious attachment can cause individuals to doubt their partner's intentions, loyalty, and love, even without concrete reasons for suspicion. Exploring these trust issues and understanding their origins is essential for healing and fostering healthier, more secure relationships.

Overanalyzing Relationship Dynamics

Anxious attachment can also lead to the tendency to overanalyze relationship dynamics. This behavior stems from a fear of losing the relationship or not being good enough for the partner. Individuals may find themselves constantly looking for signs of something wrong or their partner's feelings have changed. This hyper-vigilance can strain the relationship, creating tension where none existed and potentially leading to a self-fulfilling prophecy of relationship instability. Awareness of this tendency and its effects is crucial for mitigating its impact on the relationship's stability.

Understanding and addressing the behaviors associated with anxious attachment, such as difficulty trusting partners and overanalyzing relationship dynamics, are critical steps toward building more secure and fulfilling relationships. By acknowledging these patterns and working through them, individuals can move towards healthier attachment styles and more stable, loving relationships.

Introduction to Techniques for Managing Anxious Behaviors

Welcome to a crucial part of your journey toward understanding and transforming the anxious attachment behaviors that influence your relationships. The goal of integrating specific techniques into your daily routines is foundational to increasing self-awareness, regulating your emotional responses, and altering the negative thought patterns that often underpin anxious attachment. By dedicating time and effort to these practices, you can see profound changes in how you relate to others view yourself and your capacity for secure, fulfilling connections.

The techniques we will explore have been carefully selected for their effectiveness in addressing the unique challenges of anxious attachment. They are designed to be integrated into your daily life, ensuring the path to a more secure attachment style is accessible and sustainable. Below is a brief overview of the core techniques we will delve into mindfulness practices, journaling, and cognitive-behavioral techniques. Each of these has been chosen for its potential to offer you practical tools for managing and transforming anxious behaviors in relationships.

Mindfulness Practices

Mindfulness practices are a cornerstone of managing anxious attachment behaviors. By fostering an attitude of non-judgmental awareness, mindfulness allows you to observe your thoughts and feelings as they are, without immediate reaction or criticism. This practice is particularly beneficial for individuals with anxious attachment, as it helps in recognizing and pausing automatic responses to perceived threats in relationships, such as fear of abandonment or rejection. Through mindfulness, you can learn to sit with uncomfortable emotions without letting them dictate your actions, thereby reducing the intensity of anxiety-driven behaviors.

Journaling

Journaling is a powerful tool for self-reflection and emotional processing. It offers a private space where you can express your thoughts, fears, and desires openly, facilitating a deeper understanding of your attachment behaviors and their triggers. Regular journaling can help you track patterns in your emotional responses and the situations that ignite anxious feelings. This awareness is the first step toward changing the narrative around your attachment experiences, enabling you to identify more adaptive ways of relating to your emotions and others.

Cognitive-Behavioral Techniques

Cognitive-behavioral techniques are rooted in the understanding that our thoughts, feelings, and behaviors are interconnected. By identifying and challenging the negative thought patterns that contribute to anxious attachment—such as catastrophic thinking or mind-reading—you can begin to alter the emotional and behavioral responses that follow. These techniques often involve structured exercises to practice reframing thoughts, thus promoting more balanced and realistic perspectives on relationships and self-worth.

As we progress through this chapter, we will dive deeper into these techniques, providing practical exercises and strategies to incorporate them into your life. Remember, the path to change is a journey of small steps. By integrating these practices into your daily routine, you're not just working to manage anxious behaviors but nurturing a foundation for lasting security and fulfillment in your relationships.

Mindfulness Practices

Mindfulness is the practice of maintaining a moment-by-moment awareness of our thoughts, feelings, bodily sensations, and surrounding environment with openness, curiosity, and without judgment. It encourages us to experience the present moment fully rather than being caught up in thoughts about the past or future. This practice is particularly beneficial for individuals experiencing anxious attachment, as it can significantly reduce anxiety levels and enhance emotional regulation.

The benefits of mindfulness are manifold. It helps lower stress, improves attention, decreases emotional reactivity, and enhances cognitive flexibility. For those with anxious attachment, mindfulness can be a game-changer. It teaches you to recognize and accept your feelings of anxiety without letting them overwhelm your sense of self or dictate your actions. This acceptance and awareness can lead to a profound shift in how you experience relationships, making room for more secure and grounded interactions.

Daily Integration

Morning Routine:
Begin your day with a brief mindfulness meditation to establish a foundation of calm and presence. Allocate a few minutes each morning to sit quietly and focus on your breath or bodily sensations. As you breathe in and out, observe any thoughts or feelings that arise without judgment, simply letting them pass. This practice sets a positive tone for the day, helping you approach situations with a grounded and centered mindset.

Mindful Moments:
Integrate mindful moments throughout your day to cultivate the habit of pausing and choosing your responses rather than reacting impulsively. Take a deep breath to ground yourself before responding to conversations, especially in tension or disagreement. This brief pause allows you to respond from a place of calm and clarity rather than from anxiety or fear. You can also use these mindful moments during transitions between activities, such as before starting a new task, to maintain a continuous sense of presence throughout the day.

Mindful Listening:
Practice mindful listening in your interactions with others. This involves giving full attention to the speaker, focusing on their words without planning your response or making judgments. Notice the tendency to drift into your thoughts or formulate replies while the other person is still speaking, and gently redirect your attention back to listening. Mindful listening can significantly improve the quality of your interactions, fostering deeper empathy, understanding, and connection. It shows the speaker that they are valued and heard, which can be especially reassuring in relationships affected by anxious attachment.

Incorporating these mindfulness practices into your daily routine can transform your approach to relationships and life. You create space for more authentic, empathetic, and secure connections by cultivating presence, patience, and non-judgment.

Journaling

Journaling is a powerful tool for self-exploration and emotional processing that can be particularly beneficial for individuals with anxious attachment styles. It provides a safe, private space to express thoughts and feelings, explore your inner world, and reflect on your experiences without fear of judgment or criticism. This practice can help you identify and process emotions, understand what triggers your anxious behaviors, and gain insights into your thinking patterns and relationship reactions.

One of the key benefits of journaling is its ability to bring clarity to the complex web of thoughts and emotions that characterize anxious attachment. By regularly writing down your thoughts and feelings, you can begin to untangle the threads of your experiences, seeing more clearly the connections between your thoughts, emotions, and behaviors. This clarity can be instrumental in recognizing the habitual patterns contributing to relationship difficulties, allowing you to approach these challenges with greater awareness and intention.

Daily Integration

Emotion Tracking:
Start keeping a daily emotion journal. Each day, take a few moments to note any anxiety, insecurity, or other significant emotions, along with the context in which they occurred. Try to pinpoint what triggered these feelings, whether a particular interaction, thought, or external event. Over time, you will likely begin to see patterns in what triggers your anxious attachment behaviors, providing valuable insights into how you can begin to address and modify these responses.

Gratitude Journaling:
End your day positively by writing down three things you are grateful for. These can be small, everyday occurrences, such as a pleasant conversation, quiet reflection, or more significant events. Gratitude journaling helps shift your focus from fears and insecurities to the positive aspects of your life and relationships. This shift can foster a sense of well-being and security, countering the negative bias often experienced by those with anxious attachment.

Response Reflection:
After experiencing moments of anxiety or conflict, take some time to journal about the situation. Write down what happened and how you initially responded, and then reflect on alternative, more constructive responses you could choose in the future. This exercise is not about criticizing yourself for your reactions but exploring different ways of handling similar situations moving forward. By considering alternative responses, you begin to widen your repertoire of coping strategies, making it easier to react in more secure and healthy ways in the future.

Integrating these journaling practices into your daily routine can significantly enhance your ability to understand and manage the emotions and behaviors associated with anxious attachment. With time and consistency, journaling can become vital to your journey toward more secure and fulfilling relationships.

Cognitive-Behavioral Techniques

Cognitive-behavioral techniques are grounded in the understanding that our thoughts, emotions, and behaviors are interconnected and that we can alter our emotional responses and behaviors by changing negative thought patterns and beliefs. These methods are particularly effective for individuals with anxious attachment, as they often struggle with pervasive negative thoughts and beliefs about themselves, their relationships, and their worthiness of love and connection.

The core benefit of cognitive-behavioral techniques is their ability to help you identify, challenge, and ultimately change the distorted thought patterns that contribute to anxious attachment behaviors. By examining the accuracy of your thoughts and considering more balanced perspectives, you can reduce the intensity of your emotional responses and engage in healthier behaviors within your relationships.

Daily Integration

Thought Records:
Start by keeping a thought record. Whenever you notice yourself experiencing anxious thoughts, especially those related to your relationships, write them down. Next to each thought, list the evidence that supports and contradicts this thought. Then, try to develop a more balanced perspective that considers this evidence. This practice can help you see that

many of your anxious thoughts are not fully supported by evidence and that there are more constructive ways to view the situation.

Behavioral Experiments:
Engage in small, daily behavioral experiments to test the validity of the fears underlying your anxious thoughts. For example, if you're afraid that expressing a need will lead to rejection or conflict, try expressing a small need calmly and clearly and observe the outcome. These experiments can provide real-life evidence that challenges and modifies your inaccurate beliefs about how others will respond to your actions, helping you become more comfortable with vulnerability and open communication in your relationships.

Relaxation Techniques:
Incorporate relaxation exercises into your daily routine to help manage the physiological symptoms of anxiety that often accompany anxious attachment. Techniques such as progressive muscle relaxation, where you tense and then gradually relax different muscle groups, or guided imagery, where you visualize a calm and peaceful scene, can be very effective. Practicing these techniques can help reduce overall stress and anxiety levels, making it easier to engage in the cognitive and behavioral changes you're working toward.

Integrating these cognitive-behavioral techniques into daily life can significantly impact your journey toward more secure attachment and healthier relationships. By systematically addressing the thoughts and beliefs underpinning your anxious attachment, you can foster a greater sense of security within yourself and others.

Building a Toolkit for Change

As we conclude this chapter on managing anxious behaviors in relationships, it's important to remember that the journey toward change is deeply personal and uniquely yours. The techniques outlined in this chapter—mindfulness practices, journaling, and cognitive-behavioral techniques—serve as a starting point for building your toolkit for change. However, the most effective toolkit is personalized to fit your needs, lifestyle, and preferences. I encourage you to experiment with these techniques, combining and adapting them in ways that resonate most deeply with you and seamlessly integrate into your daily routine.

Developing new habits and changing long-standing anxious attachment patterns is a process that unfolds over time. It requires a growth mindset—patience, practice, and persistence. Remember, progress is not always linear; there will be days when everything seems to click and others where old patterns feel inescapable. This is a natural part of the learning and growth process. Embrace these fluctuations with compassion and curiosity, seeing them as opportunities to deepen your understanding and refine your approach.

As you progress, stay open to adapting your techniques as you grow and evolve. Your needs and circumstances will change, and your toolkit should evolve to reflect these changes. For instance, you might find mindfulness more beneficial during certain phases, while at other times, journaling or cognitive-behavioral strategies may offer greater insights and relief. The key is to remain flexible and responsive to your evolving journey.

Finally, remember that support is a crucial component of change. If integrating these practices into your life becomes challenging, or if you find yourself struggling to navigate the complexities of anxious attachment on your own, seeking support from a therapist or joining a support group can provide valuable guidance and encouragement. These resources can offer a supportive community and professional expertise to help you navigate the path toward more secure and fulfilling relationships.

Building a toolkit for change is an empowering step towards transforming your relationship with yourself and others. With each technique you integrate and each small change you make, you are laying the groundwork for a more secure, confident, and connected way of being.

Identifying Triggers and Emotional Responses

For individuals with an anxious attachment style, navigating the complexities of relationships can often feel like sailing through a storm without a compass. Emotional triggers—specific events or behaviors from others that provoke a strong emotional response—play a significant role in this experience. Recognizing these triggers and understanding the typical emotional responses they evoke is crucial for managing anxious attachment. This section delves into common triggers, the nature of emotional responses to these triggers, and strategies for cultivating mindfulness and healthier response mechanisms.

The Role of Self-Awareness

Self-awareness is the cornerstone of identifying and managing anxious attachment behaviors. It involves an ongoing process of reflection to recognize the specific situations, comments, or actions that trigger anxiety and insecurity in relationships. This self-awareness allows individuals to step back and observe their reactions objectively, setting the stage for transforming these automatic responses into more deliberate and healthy choices.

Common Triggers for Anxious Attachment

Several scenarios commonly trigger anxiety in individuals with an anxious attachment style:

Perceived Distance or Disengagement: This can be as subtle as a partner being distracted or as significant as choosing to spend time apart. For someone with anxious attachment, these situations can quickly be interpreted as signs of waning interest or affection.

Lack of Reassurance: Failing to receive regular affirmations of love and commitment can trigger deep-seated fears of abandonment and unworthiness.

Conflicts and Criticism: Arguments or critical remarks may be perceived not as isolated incidents but as indicators of a flawed relationship or personal inadequacy.

Typical Emotional Responses

The emotional responses to these triggers are intense and multifaceted, including:

Anxiety and Fear: A visceral fear of losing the relationship or being deemed unlovable, often accompanied by physical symptoms of anxiety.

A compulsion to Seek Closeness or Reassurance: An overwhelming need to restore proximity and security through reassurance from the partner, which can manifest as clingy or demanding behaviors.

Understanding Healthy vs. Unhealthy Emotional Responses

Differentiating between healthy and unhealthy emotional responses is key to managing anxious attachment. Healthy responses involve constructively expressing needs and concerns, seeking clarity, and respecting boundaries. Unhealthy responses, conversely, may involve excessive reassurance-seeking, interpreting neutral actions as negative without evidence, or allowing fear to dictate behaviors in a way that undermines personal well-being and relationship health.

Practical Tips for Tracking and Reflecting

To become more mindful of triggers and manage emotional responses effectively, consider these practical tips:

Maintain a Reaction Journal: Document instances when you feel triggered, noting the situation, your immediate emotional response, and how you chose to react. Over time, patterns will emerge, offering insights into your triggers and typical responses.

Practice Mindfulness: Mindfulness exercises can help you stay present and grounded, reducing the intensity of emotional reactions and providing space to choose how to respond more thoughtfully.

Seek Feedback: Sometimes, discussing your perceptions and reactions with a trusted friend or partner is beneficial. Their perspectives can offer valuable insights and help you gauge the accuracy of your interpretations.

Identifying triggers and understanding the emotional responses they provoke is a fundamental aspect of managing anxious attachment. Individuals can navigate their triggers more effectively by cultivating self-awareness and employing practical strategies for reflection and response, fostering healthier emotional dynamics within themselves and their relationships. This journey towards self-understanding and growth mitigates the impact of anxious attachment and paves the way for more secure and fulfilling connections.

Chapter Exercises

Anxious Attachment Behavior Log Exercise

Objective:

This exercise aims to increase your self-awareness regarding anxious attachment behaviors by maintaining a detailed log. Recognizing these moments is the first step towards understanding your triggers and developing healthier relational patterns.

Materials Needed:

- A journal or digital notepad dedicated to your behavior log.
- A pen or digital device for recording entries.

Steps to Maintain Your Behavior Log:

Step 1: Understand Anxious Attachment Behaviors
Begin by familiarizing yourself with common anxious attachment behaviors, such as needing constant reassurance, fear of abandonment, difficulty trusting partners, or overanalyzing your relationships.

Step 2: Daily Logging
At the end of each day, take a moment to reflect on your interactions and feelings. Record any instances where you recognize anxious attachment behaviors. Note the situation, your feelings, reactions, and any triggers if identifiable.

Step 3: Identify Patterns
Review your entries after logging in for a week or two to identify patterns or common triggers. This could be specific situations, words, actions by others, or internal states like tiredness or stress.

Step 4: Reflect on Underlying Needs

For each identified behavior, try to understand the underlying need or fear. Is it a need for security, fear of losing someone, or something else? This understanding can help in addressing these needs more healthily.

Step 5: Develop Coping Strategies

Based on your reflections, outline healthier coping strategies or ways to communicate your needs without falling back on anxious behaviors. This might include self-soothing techniques, clear communication of needs, or seeking reassurance in a balanced way.

Example Entry:

- Date: September 15
- Situation: Partner was late to our dinner date without sending a message.
- Feelings: Anxiety, abandonment, fear, anger.
- Reaction: Sent multiple texts asking where they were and felt relieved when they arrived, but I didn't express my feelings directly.
- Trigger: Lack of communication leading to uncertainty.
- Underlying Need: Need for reassurance and communication to feel secure.
- Coping Strategy: Discuss the importance of communication with my partner and practice patience and trust in their commitment.

Conclusion:

Maintaining an Anxious Attachment Behavior Log can offer profound insights into your relational dynamics and personal triggers. This exercise encourages awareness and empowers you to actively build more secure attachment patterns in your relationships.

Anxiety Management Techniques Exercise

Objective:

This exercise is crafted to equip you with effective anxiety management techniques tailored specifically for moments when relationship challenges arise. The goal is to help you navigate these situations more calmly and clearly.

Materials Needed:

- A comfortable and quiet space for practice.
- A journal or digital device for noting down reflections and observations.

Techniques and Application:

Technique 1: Deep Breathing
Description: Deep breathing helps to calm the nervous system and reduce stress.

How to Apply: Whenever you feel anxiety creeping up due to a relationship issue, pause and take deep, slow breaths. Inhale deeply through your nose, hold for a moment, and exhale slowly through your mouth.

Example: Practice deep breathing to center yourself before addressing a sensitive topic with your partner.

Technique 2: Mindfulness Meditation
Description: Mindfulness meditation focuses on being present in the moment, which can help reduce anxiety.

How to Apply: Dedicate a few minutes daily to sit quietly and focus on your breath. When your mind wanders to anxious thoughts, gently bring your attention back to your breathing.

Example: Practice mindfulness meditation in the morning to start your day with a calm mind, better preparing you for future relationship challenges.

Technique 3: Progressive Muscle Relaxation
Description: This technique involves tensing and relaxing different muscle groups to reduce anxiety.

How to Apply: Start from your toes and up to your head. Tense each muscle group for a few seconds and then relax it. Notice the contrast between tension and relaxation.

Example: Use progressive muscle relaxation before a difficult conversation to release tension in your body and approach the discussion more calmly.

Technique 4: Positive Affirmations

Description: Positive affirmations can shift your mindset from anxiety to confidence and calm.

How to Apply: Create a list of positive affirmations that resonate with you and your relationship goals. Repeat these affirmations to yourself, especially during challenging times.

Example: Affirmations like "I am capable of handling conflict with kindness and assertiveness" can empower you before addressing issues with your partner.

Technique 5: Journaling

Description: Writing down your thoughts and feelings can help you process anxiety and gain perspective.

How to Apply: Keep a journal to regularly write about your anxieties related to your relationship. Reflect on what triggers these feelings and how you respond to them.

Example: Journal about your fears of abandonment, noting specific situations that trigger these fears and exploring healthier ways to respond.

Reflect and Grow:

After trying these techniques, reflect on their effectiveness. Note any changes in your anxiety levels and your ability to manage relationship challenges. Over time, you may find certain techniques more beneficial than others. Customize your approach based on what works best for you.

Conclusion:

Employing these anxiety management techniques can significantly improve your ability to face relationship challenges with a more balanced and calm approach. Remember, the goal is not to eliminate anxiety but to learn how to manage it effectively, fostering healthier and more resilient relationships.

Fear Facing Exercise

Objective:

This exercise allows you to face and articulate the fears that linger in the corners of your relationships. By openly acknowledging these fears, you set the stage for understanding and confronting them with your partner or within yourself, fostering a deeper connection and mutual support.

Materials Needed:

- A quiet, comfortable space where you feel safe to reflect and be honest.
- A notebook or any digital device where you can record your thoughts.
- An open heart and an open mind.

Let's Dive In:

Step 1: Identifying Your Fears
Start by taking a deep breath. Allow yourself to reflect on the fears you have concerning your relationships. These could range from fear of abandonment, not being good enough, and fear of conflict to fear of losing independence. Write these fears down as they come to you without judgment.

Step 2: Deep Dive into Each Fear
For each fear you've listed, write a brief explanation of why you think this fear exists. What experiences, conversations, or observations have contributed to this fear? This step helps in understanding the root of each fear.

Step 3: Discuss Openly
If you're comfortable, select a time to discuss these fears with your partner or a trusted friend. The goal isn't to solve these fears immediately but to share them openly. If you're reflecting individually, consider how acknowledging these fears makes you feel and what steps you might take to address them.

Step 4: Confronting Fears Together

After sharing, discuss ways you might help each other confront and overcome these fears. This could involve setting specific goals, offering reassurances, or developing new communication strategies. If you're working through this individually, outline actions to challenge these fears, such as self-care practices, seeking therapy, or engaging in activities that boost your confidence and sense of security.

Examples:

Fear: "My partner will find someone better and leave me."

Why: "Because I've been abandoned before in past relationships."

Open Discussion: Sharing this fear with your partner might lead to conversations about trust, reassurance, and the unique strengths you both bring to the relationship.

Confronting Together: Agree on daily affirmations or reassurances that address this fear, or perhaps attend couples therapy to work through these insecurities.

Fear: "I worry that voicing my needs will push my partner away."

Why: "My concerns were dismissed in the past, making me feel needy and burdensome."

Open Discussion: Expressing this fear can open the door to establishing healthier communication patterns where both partners feel heard and valued.

Confronting Together: Create a 'safe words' system for when either of you feels overwhelmed in discussions, ensuring everyone's needs are communicated and respected.

Reflection:

After going through this exercise, take some time to reflect on what it felt like to name and share your fears. Did any insights emerge? How did discussing these fears affect your relationship or your understanding of yourself?

Conclusion:

Facing your fears is a courageous step towards building stronger, more secure relationships. Remember, it's okay to have fears, but confronting them openly can transform them into opportunities for growth and deeper connection. Keep this exercise as a tool to revisit whenever new fears arise, knowing you're building a foundation of trust and understanding each time you face them.

Secure Attachment Role Models Exercise

Objective

This exercise aims to guide you in identifying and reflecting on the qualities of secure attachment as shown by role models in your life or the public domain. The goal is to inspire you to embody these qualities yourself.

Materials Needed

- A journal or digital document for writing reflections
- A pen or pencil if you're using a physical journal

Instructions

Introduction to Secure Attachment

Start by understanding what secure attachment looks like. It's characterized by trust, a positive view of oneself and others, comfort with closeness and independence, and effective communication and conflict resolution skills.

Identification of Role Models

- **Personal Life:** Think of individuals in your circle who embody secure attachment qualities. These might be family members, friends, teachers, or mentors known for their trust, empathy, independence, and comfort with intimacy.
- **Public Figures:** Also, consider public figures or characters from literature, film, or television who demonstrate secure attachment traits. Identify those who display healthy, balanced relationships, communicate openly, and balance intimacy with independence.

Journaling Exercise

1. **Description of Role Models:** For each role model you've identified, write down the qualities that signify secure attachment. Focus on the specific behaviors and traits that resonate with you.
2. **Examples of Secure Attachment Behaviors:** Note how these role models show secure attachment in their actions. Include how they handle communication in challenging times, their ways of offering support, or how they balance individuality and closeness.
3. **Reflection on Influence:** Reflect on the impact these role models have had on your perception of relationships and attachment. Have these observations motivated you to adapt or strive for similar behaviors in your own life?

Action Plan

- **Qualities to Cultivate:** From your reflections, pinpoint the secure attachment qualities you wish to develop further. List concrete steps you can take to embody these traits.

- **Strategies for Growth:** Draft a plan to integrate these secure attachment behaviors into your life. Consider practicing open communication, enhancing self-esteem, establishing healthy boundaries, or fostering relationships that promote mutual respect and independence.

Examples

- **Personal Role Model:** "My friend Alex manages disagreements calmly and clearly, showing the essence of active listening and compromise. Inspired by Alex, I'm committed to improving my active listening skills and sharing my needs and feelings more openly."

- **Public Figure:** "Michelle Obama exemplifies secure attachment through her self-assuredness, open communication, and partnership. Her balance of personal ambitions and relational roles motivates me to bolster my self-confidence and communicate my aspirations and concerns more transparently."

Reflection and Review

Regularly revisit your role models and admired qualities, assessing your growth and evolving insights. This practice encourages continuous reflection and adjustment as you progress toward secure attachment.

Conclusion

This exercise is a foundation for recognizing and adopting secure attachment qualities in your personal development. It promotes persistent reflection, growth, and the acknowledgment that nurturing secure attachment is an ongoing process.

Chapter 4

Building Self-Awareness

Introduction

This chapter embarks on a transformative journey, illuminating the vital role of self-awareness in overcoming anxious attachment and fostering secure, fulfilling relationships. At the heart of anxious attachment lies a web of deeply ingrained beliefs and early experiences that shape our interactions and emotional responses in adult relationships. Unraveling these layers to understand the roots of our attachment style is not just enlightening; it's a crucial step toward healing and growth. This chapter introduces exercises and reflections designed to guide you through the intricate process of mapping your attachment history, identifying core beliefs about yourself, others, and relationships, and confronting the early signs of anxious attachment.

As we delve into the origins of our attachment behaviors and the patterns of need and neglect that have influenced us, it's important to acknowledge that this exploration can stir up painful memories and emotions. Yet, recognizing and accepting these parts of our history is more than half the battle in beginning to heal and transform them. The exercises in this chapter, ranging from mindfulness practices to strategies for self-compassion, are carefully curated to support you in this sensitive journey. They aim to foster a profound level of self-understanding and acceptance, equipping you with the tools to address and reframe self-critical thoughts and beliefs gently.

It's essential to approach this journey with patience and kindness towards oneself, understanding that self-awareness is a powerful catalyst for change. By becoming attuned to the nuances of our emotional world and the narratives that have shaped us, we can start to navigate toward more secure attachment patterns. This chapter is about uncovering past pains and laying the groundwork for a future where secure relationships and self-compassion pave the way for a life of confidence and emotional security.

The Importance of Self-Awareness in Overcoming Anxious Attachment

Self-awareness stands as a crucial element in the journey toward overcoming anxious attachment. It involves a deep understanding of one's emotions, thoughts, behaviors, and the underlying patterns that drive them. This chapter emphasizes the importance of self-awareness in identifying and modifying the anxious attachment behaviors that hinder personal growth and the development of healthy relationships.

Building self-awareness is foundational in managing anxious attachment effectively. It allows individuals to recognize the triggers that provoke anxiety and insecurity within relationships, offering insights into how these reactions can be transformed into responses that foster security and trust. Understanding oneself can challenge the fears and assumptions that fuel anxious attachment, paving the way for more secure attachment patterns to emerge.

Overview of Exercises and Reflections in This Chapter

This chapter presents a series of exercises and reflections designed to enhance self-awareness. These activities are geared towards helping individuals explore their attachment style, understand the origins of their anxiety within relationships, and identify strategies for fostering a sense of security and self-worth. Through guided introspection, journaling exercises, and mindfulness practices, readers will gain valuable tools to understand themselves and their relational dynamics better, ultimately leading to profound personal growth and healthier relationships.

Section 1: Exploring Personal History and Beliefs

Mapping Your Attachment History

This section encourages individuals to embark on reflective exercises to trace the origins of their anxious attachment behaviors. By delving into past relationships and significant life events, readers can uncover the patterns and experiences that have contributed to developing their anxious attachment style.

It is crucial to identify the key relationships and experiences that have influenced their attachment style. This could involve examining the dynamics of parental relationships, past romantic partnerships, and other significant interpersonal connections. Recognizing these influential factors offers valuable insights into why one may experience anxiety in relationships and how these patterns of attachment are formed.

This process not only aids in identifying the roots of anxious attachment but also sets the groundwork for healing and developing healthier relationship dynamics.

Life Timeline Exercise: Understanding Your Attachment Style

Objective:

This exercise aims to visually represent your life timeline, focusing on significant events and their influence on your attachment style. By examining these moments, you'll gain insight into the development of your relational patterns. This understanding is pivotal for nurturing secure attachments and enhancing your interpersonal relationships.

Materials Needed:

- A large sheet of paper or a digital document (e.g., a word processor or a drawing app).
- Colored pens, markers, or digital tools for color-coding (optional).
- A journal or notebook for deeper reflection.

Instructions:

1. **Setup:** Find a peaceful, uninterrupted space conducive to introspection. Prepare your timeline medium (paper or digital) and writing or drawing instruments.

2. **Drawing the Timeline:** Sketch a horizontal line across your paper or digital canvas. This represents your life's journey from birth to the present. Mark significant life stages along this line (childhood, adolescence, adulthood, etc.), indicating your age or the year these phases occurred.

3. ***Identifying Key Events:*** Reflect on and list events that have profoundly impacted you. These can include joyous, traumatic, or transformative experiences. Examples of significant events to consider are:
   - ***Family Dynamics:*** Parents' divorce and the arrival of a new sibling.
   - ***Relationship Milestones:*** First love, a significant breakup, meeting a life partner.
   - ***Educational and Career Achievements:*** Graduating, landing a dream job, experiencing job loss.
   - ***Health Challenges:*** Personal illnesses, caring for a sick family member. Moves and Transitions: Relocating to a new city or country, changing schools.

4. ***Mapping the Events:*** Place each identified event on the timeline where it belongs chronologically. Please write a short note beside each event detailing what happened and its immediate emotional impact on you.

5. ***Exploring Attachment Impacts:*** Before each event, ponder and note how it might have shaped your views on trust, independence, and emotional intimacy in relationships. Ask yourself: How did this experience influence my sense of security or insecurity in relationships? How did it affect my approach to closeness and distance with others?

6. ***Journaling for Depth:*** With your timeline as a reference, journal about the trends you observe in your relational dynamics over the years. Discuss recurring emotions, reactions, or beliefs about relationships that your timeline reveals.

7. ***Forward Reflection:*** Reflect on insights from this exercise and how they might inform your future relationship goals and approaches. Identify specific steps you can take to foster a more secure attachment style moving forward.

This exercise is a reflective journey through your past, clarifying how pivotal events have molded your relationship approach. Creating and analyzing your life timeline can unlock a deeper understanding of your attachment style, revealing pathways to more secure and enriching connections.

Explanation:

This life timeline exercise is grounded in the principles of attachment theory, which suggests that our early experiences with caregivers shape our expectations and behaviors in adult relationships. By mapping out significant life events, you can explore the origins of your beliefs and behaviors around attachment. This exploration can illuminate patterns that may be contributing to current relationship dynamics. Understanding these patterns provides a foundation for intentional change, guiding you toward healthier, more secure attachment styles. The examples are intended to prompt the recollection of similar impactful moments in your life, aiding in a comprehensive, enlightening, and transformative self-assessment.

Understanding Your Belief Systems

Exercises to uncover core beliefs about self, others, and relationships are vital for those looking to understand and navigate their attachment styles. These exercises help identify the deep-seated beliefs that influence how individuals perceive themselves and their interactions with others.

Understanding these belief systems is crucial because they significantly impact one's attachment style and behaviors. Core beliefs can shape how individuals respond to closeness, intimacy, and conflict within relationships. Individuals can alter their attachment patterns toward more secure and healthy relationships by exploring and challenging these beliefs.

Core Values Clarification Exercise: Aligning Personal Values with Behaviors

Objective:

This exercise aims to help you identify, list, and prioritize your core personal values and explore how these values align with your current behaviors. Understanding and living in accordance with your core values can enhance your sense of well-being, decision-making, and integrity in daily life.

Materials Needed:

- Pen and paper or a digital document/note-taking app.
- A quiet space for reflection.

Instructions:

1. **Identification of Core Values:** List values that resonate with you deeply. These could include honesty, compassion, freedom, family, success, creativity, or integrity. Aim to list around 10-20 values initially.

2. **Examples of Values:**
    - Honesty: Valuing open and truthful communication.
    - Compassion: Showing empathy and kindness towards others.
    - Freedom: Prioritizing autonomy in your personal and professional life.
    - Family: Placing importance on family relationships and time spent together.
    - Success: Striving for achievement and recognition in your endeavors.
    - Creativity: Valuing innovative thinking and expression in various forms.
    - Integrity: Acting consistently with your beliefs and values.

3. **Prioritizing Your Values:** Review your list and begin to prioritize these values. Consider which values are non-negotiable and which might be secondary. This can be challenging but aim to identify your top 5 core values.

4. **Alignment with Current Behaviors:** For each of your top 5 values, write down how your current behaviors and life choices align with these values. Be honest with yourself about areas of congruence and discrepancy.

5. **Setting Intentions for Greater Alignment:** *Identify* specific actions or changes you can make to live more in alignment with your core values. This might involve setting new goals, altering certain behaviors, or changing lifestyles.

6. **Reflection and Adjustment:** Reflect on this process and how it makes you feel. Consider setting regular check-ins with yourself to revisit your values and alignment, as personal values can evolve over time.

Clarifying and living according to your core values can significantly impact your life's fulfillment and authenticity. This exercise is a step towards greater self-awareness and alignment between your values and daily actions, contributing to a more coherent and meaningful life.

Explanation:

Core Values Clarification is foundational in personal development and psychotherapy, particularly in approaches like Acceptance and Commitment Therapy (ACT). It helps individuals to live more authentically and to make choices that resonate with their deeper selves. When actions and values are aligned, individuals often experience increased satisfaction, decreased stress, and greater overall well-being. This exercise encourages introspection and deliberate living, ensuring that your life path reflects what truly matters to you.

Belief System Mapping: Core Beliefs About Relationships

Objective:

This exercise aims to help you identify and map out your core beliefs about relationships, including their origins and how they influence your current relationship dynamics. By understanding these foundational beliefs, you can begin to challenge and adjust any hindering your ability to form secure and fulfilling connections.

Materials Needed:

- A large sheet of paper or a digital drawing/document app.
- Writing or drawing tools (pens, markers, or digital equivalents).
- A journal or notebook for additional reflections.

Instructions:

1. **Preparation:** Find a quiet space where you can focus without distractions. Prepare your materials, choosing a digital or paper format for your mapping exercise.

2. **Identifying Core Beliefs:** Reflect on the statements you believe to be true about relationships. These can range from beliefs about trust, commitment, and love to expectations of conflict, betrayal, and abandonment.
   Examples of core beliefs might include:
   - Relationships always end in hurt.
   - I must be perfect to be loved.
   - Showing vulnerability is a sign of weakness.
   - Conflict means the relationship is failing.

3. ***Mapping Out Origins:*** For each core belief, trace its origin. Consider childhood experiences, influential relationships, societal messages, and significant events that might have contributed to these beliefs. Draw lines or arrows from each belief to briefly describe its origin. For example, the belief 'I must be perfect to be loved' may stem from a childhood where parental approval was conditional on achievements.

4. ***Reflecting on Impact:*** Next to each belief and its origin, note how this belief has impacted your relationships. Has it led to avoidance, clinginess, or sabotaging relationships? Reflect on specific examples.

5. ***Challenging and Adjusting Beliefs:*** With your beliefs and their impacts outlined, consider which ones are unhelpful or unrealistic. Write down alternative, more adaptive beliefs. For example, instead of 'Conflict means the relationship is failing,' consider 'Conflict is an opportunity for growth.'

6. ***Journaling for Deeper Insight:*** Use your journal to reflect on this exercise. How do you feel about the beliefs you've identified and the new ones you're considering? How can you start integrating these new beliefs into your life?

7. ***Action Plan:*** Create a small, actionable plan to challenge and adjust your core beliefs in daily life. This might include mindfulness of when old beliefs surface, practicing new responses, or seeking feedback from trusted others.

This mapping exercise provides a visual and reflective exploration of the core beliefs shaping your relationship approach. By identifying, understanding, and beginning to adjust these beliefs, you pave the way for healthier, more secure connections.

Explanation:

Belief System Mapping is a powerful tool rooted in cognitive-behavioral therapy (CBT) principles. It helps individuals see the connection between their thoughts (in this case, core beliefs about relationships), emotions, and behaviors. Understanding this linkage is crucial because core beliefs act as filters through which we interpret the world around us. If these beliefs are distorted or negative, they can lead to maladaptive behaviors and emotions, particularly in the context of relationships. Challenging and adjusting these core beliefs can shift how you feel and act in relationships, leading to more positive outcomes and greater satisfaction. This exercise encourages introspection and self-awareness, vital components of personal growth and emotional intelligence in relationships.

Section 2: The Roots of Anxious Attachment

Identifying Early Signs of Anxious Attachment

To understand the roots of anxious attachment, we embark on a journey of self-discovery, beginning with the earliest memories of anxiety and fear in relationships. Reflective prompts guide you to explore those pivotal moments when your attachment system first showed signs of distress. Examining these early signs gives you invaluable insights into the patterns shaping your emotional landscape.

Analyzing past experiences of emotional needs being met or neglected is crucial in understanding the development of anxious attachment. This section delves into the complex dynamics of need fulfillment and neglect, uncovering how these experiences have contributed to your attachment style. Through guided analysis, you'll learn to identify how your emotional needs were acknowledged or overlooked, shedding light on the patterns that contribute to your current relationship dynamics.

This exploration, while potentially challenging, is a vital step towards healing. By confronting and understanding these early experiences, you can begin to heal the wounds of the past and pave the way for more secure and fulfilling relationships in the future.

Exercise: Reflective Prompts to Explore Early Memories of Anxiety and Fear in Relationships

Instructions:

1. Find a Comfortable Space: Begin by finding a quiet and comfortable space where you feel safe to explore your thoughts and feelings.

2. Breathing Exercise: Start with a brief breathing exercise to center yourself. Take deep, slow breaths to ground your presence in the moment.

3. Reflective Prompts: Use the prompts below to guide your exploration. Write your responses in your journal or notebook. Take time with each prompt, allowing yourself to engage with your memories and emotions fully.

- ***Prompt 1***: Recall the earliest memory you have of feeling anxious or fearful in a relationship. This could be with a parent, sibling, friend, or any significant person in your early life. Describe the situation and how you felt.

- ***Prompt 2:*** Think about a time in your childhood or adolescence when you felt your emotional needs were neglected. What did you need then, and how did the lack of fulfillment make you feel?

- ***Prompt 3:*** Reflect on a relationship in your early life where you experienced a strong fear of abandonment or rejection. How did this fear manifest in your behavior and feelings towards the person?

- ***Prompt 4:*** Consider the patterns of attachment in your family. How did the adults around you express love, affection, and support? How did these expressions (or lack thereof) shape your expectations of relationships?

- ***Prompt 5***: Identify a turning point in understanding your attachment behaviors. When did you first recognize that your early experiences influenced your adult relationships?

4. ***Reflection and Compassion:*** After completing the prompts, reflect on your responses. Offer yourself compassion and understanding for your experiences and recognize the strength it takes to confront these memories.

5. ***Closing Thought:*** Acknowledge your progress by engaging with these prompts. Remember that understanding your past is a significant step towards healing and growth in your relationships.

Note: This exercise may bring up strong emotions. If at any point you feel overwhelmed, it's okay to take a break and return when you feel ready. Consider seeking support from a therapist or counselor if you find these reflections particularly challenging to navigate independently.

Section 3: Mindfulness and Self-Awareness

Introduction to Mindfulness

Mindfulness is being fully present and engaged at the moment, aware of our thoughts, emotions, and sensations without judgment. It's about observing our inner and outer experiences with openness and curiosity. This ancient practice, rooted in Buddhist traditions, has gained widespread recognition for its benefits in reducing stress, enhancing emotional regulation, and improving overall mental health. In the context of attachment and relationships, mindfulness is a powerful tool for enhancing self-awareness, allowing individuals to recognize and understand their emotional responses, triggers, and behavior patterns.

Basics of Mindfulness and Its Benefits for Enhancing Self-Awareness

The essence of mindfulness lies in its simplicity —the art of paying attention to purpose. We can observe our thoughts and feelings without becoming entangled by directing our focus to the present moment. This practice fosters a deeper understanding of ourselves, highlighting the transient nature of our emotions and thoughts. As a result, mindfulness enhances our self-awareness, enabling us to identify anxious attachment behaviors and address them more effectively. It helps break the cycle of reactivity that often characterizes anxious attachment, encouraging a more balanced and reflective approach to relationship challenges.

Cultivating Presence in Relationships

Being present in our relationships means listening, understanding, and responding to our partners with full attention and empathy. Mindfulness enhances our focus on the present interaction, fostering deeper connections and emotional intimacy. It teaches us to respond rather than react, allowing for more thoughtful and compassionate communication. Strategies for cultivating presence in relationships include:

- **Active Listening:** Engaging fully with what the other person is saying without formulating a response while they are speaking. This involves hearing their words and paying attention to non-verbal cues such as tone of voice and body language.

- **Pausing Before Reacting:** Taking a moment to breathe and reflect before responding in conversations, especially in emotionally charged situations. This pause can help prevent knee-jerk reactions that may escalate conflicts.

- **Shared Mindfulness Practices:** Engaging in mindfulness exercises, such as meditating, can enhance mutual understanding and empathy, creating a shared space of awareness and connection.

Mindfulness Meditation for Awareness: Enhancing Self-Awareness Through Guided Practice

Objective:

This exercise is aimed at enhancing self-awareness through the practice of mindfulness meditation. Focusing on guided meditations can cultivate a deeper sense of presence, understand your thoughts and emotions more clearly, and foster calm awareness in daily life.

Materials Needed:

- A quiet and comfortable place to sit or lie down.
- Optional: Access to guided mindfulness meditation resources (apps, online videos, or audio tracks).
- A timer if not using a guided resource.

Instructions:

1. **Preparation:** Find a quiet space where you will not be disturbed for the duration of the meditation. This could be a comfortable chair, cushion, or any spot where you can sit or lie down comfortably. Set your intention for the practice. It might be as simple as wanting to be present or to explore your inner experience with curiosity.

2. **Choosing a Guided Meditation:** If using a guided meditation resource, select a meditation focused on self-awareness. This could be a body scan, breathing meditation, or any practice directing inward attention. If not using a guided resource, set your timer for a manageable duration to start, such as 5-10 minutes.

3. ***Engaging in Meditation:*** Begin the meditation by following the guide's instructions or, if meditating independently, by closing your eyes and bringing your attention to your breath. Notice the sensations of breathing in and out. When your mind wanders, gently acknowledge where it went and return your focus to the breath.

4. ***Deepening Awareness:*** As you meditate, observe thoughts, feelings, or sensations that arise without judgment. The goal is to witness your experience as it is, not to change it. Use the guidance to explore different aspects of self-awareness, whether it's noticing bodily sensations, observing thoughts, or feeling emotions.

5. ***Concluding the Meditation:*** When the meditation ends, take a moment to notice the state of your mind and body. Reflect on any changes in your awareness or mood. Gently open your eyes and transition back to your day, carrying the sense of presence and awareness cultivated during the meditation.

Mindfulness meditation is a powerful tool for enhancing self-awareness. Regular practice can help you become more attuned to your internal world, leading to greater clarity, emotional regulation, and a deeper sense of peace in your daily life.

Explanation:

Mindfulness meditation encourages a state of active, open attention to the present. Practicing regularly can significantly improve self-awareness by helping individuals become more conscious of their thoughts, feelings, and bodily sensations in a non-judgmental way. This heightened awareness can lead to better self-understanding, improved emotional intelligence, and increased capacity to respond to life's challenges calmly and clearly.

Section 4: Strategies for Self-Compassion

Understanding Self-Compassion

Self-compassion is treating oneself with the same kindness, concern, and support one would offer a good friend. It involves recognizing our shared humanity understanding that suffering and personal inadequacy are part of the human experience. Dr. Kristin Neff, a leading researcher in the field, outlines three elements of self-compassion: self-kindness, common humanity, and mindfulness. These components encourage us to be gentle with ourselves during times of failure or pain, to remember that we are not alone in our struggles, and to hold our experiences in balanced awareness.

The Role of Self-Compassion in Healing and Growth

Self-compassion plays a crucial role in emotional healing and personal growth. It allows individuals to navigate difficult emotions and challenging situations gracefully and understanding. By applying self-compassion, we can shift our perspective from isolation and self-criticism to connection and self-support. This shift enhances our relationship with ourselves and improves our interactions with others, fostering a more compassionate and understanding environment.

Differences Between Self-Compassion and Self-Criticism

While self-compassion involves treating oneself with kindness and understanding, self-criticism judges oneself harshly for perceived failures or shortcomings. Self-criticism can lead to increased stress, anxiety, and depression, creating a cycle of negative self-talk and emotional distress. In contrast, self-compassion offers a way out of this cycle, promoting emotional resilience, well-being, and a more compassionate inner dialogue. By recognizing the destructive nature of self-criticism and embracing self-compassion, individuals can begin to heal and foster a more positive and nurturing relationship with themselves.

Addressing Self-Critical Thoughts

Self-critical thoughts and beliefs can significantly hinder personal happiness and relationship satisfaction. These internal narratives often stem from past experiences, societal expectations, or personal insecurities, reinforcing negative views about ourselves and our capabilities. However, by applying specific techniques, we can identify, challenge, and transform these self-critical thoughts into more positive and supportive beliefs.

Techniques to Identify and Challenge Self-Critical Thoughts and Beliefs

1. Mindfulness and Observation: Begin by cultivating an awareness of your thought patterns. Mindfulness practice can help you observe your thoughts without getting caught up. When you notice a self-critical thought, acknowledge it without judgment and gently redirect your focus to something more constructive or neutral.

2. Thought Recording: Keep a thought diary to document instances of self-criticism. Note the situation, the thought, the emotions it evokes, and the behavior it prompts. This record can help you identify patterns and triggers of your self-critical thoughts.

3. Questioning the Evidence: Challenge your self-critical thoughts by examining the evidence for and against them. Ask yourself, "What evidence do I have that this thought is true? What evidence contradicts this thought?" This technique can help you develop a more balanced perspective.

4. Reframing Negative Thoughts: Once you've identified and questioned your self-critical thoughts, reframe them in a more positive or realistic light. For example, instead of thinking, "I always mess things up," you might reframe it to, "I've made mistakes, but I also have many successes. I can learn from my mistakes and improve."

5. Compassion Exercises: Practice speaking to yourself as you would to a dear friend facing a similar situation. What would you say to them? How would you support them? Applying this same compassion to yourself can help soften self-criticism and foster self-kindness.

6. Identifying Core Beliefs: Some self-critical thoughts are rooted in deeper core beliefs about ourselves, such as "I am not good enough" or "I am unlovable." Identifying these can help you understand the source of your self-criticism and address it more effectively.

7. Professional Support: Sometimes, self-critical thoughts are deeply ingrained and challenging to change independently. In such cases, working with a therapist or counselor can provide the support and guidance needed to address and transform these thoughts.

By actively engaging with these techniques, you can shift from self-criticism towards a more supportive and compassionate internal dialogue. This shift enhances your relationship with yourself and can improve your interactions and relationships with others, contributing to a more fulfilling and contented life.

Self-Compassion Letters: Writing to Oneself in Times of Stress or Self-Doubt

Objective:

This exercise aims to cultivate self-compassion by writing letters to oneself during stress, failure, or self-doubt. By addressing oneself with kindness, understanding, and support, you can develop a more compassionate inner voice, enhance emotional resilience, and reduce negative self-judgment.

Materials Needed:

- Writing materials (pen and paper) or a digital device for typing.
- A quiet, comfortable space for reflection.

Instructions:

1. *Identify a Triggering Event*: Consider a recent event or situation that triggered feelings of stress, inadequacy, or self-doubt. This could be a mistake at work, a personal setback, or any moment you were harshly self-critical.

2. *Writing the Letter:* Address the letter to yourself, starting with a compassionate greeting, such as 'Dear [Your Name],' Acknowledge Your Feelings: Clearly express the emotions you're experiencing. Be honest and allow yourself to feel these emotions without judgment.
   - *Offer Understanding and Compassion:* Write about the situation with kindness and understanding. Acknowledge that everyone makes mistakes and faces challenges.
   - *Provide Comfort and Encouragement:* Offer words of comfort and encouragement. Remind yourself of your strengths and past successes.
   - *Commit to Supportive Actions:* Conclude by committing to specific actions to support yourself moving forward.

3. *Reflection After Writing:* After finishing your letter, take a few moments to reflect on the process and how it made you feel. Consider the benefits of being compassionate towards yourself.

Writing self-compassion letters is a powerful practice for developing kindness towards oneself, especially in challenging times. Regularly engaging in this exercise can build a more supportive and understanding relationship with yourself, contributing to greater emotional well-being and resilience.

Explanation:

Self-compassion involves treating oneself with the same kindness, concern, and support one would show a good friend. Research in psychology, particularly the work of Dr. Kristin Neff, has shown that self-compassion can lead to increased happiness, resilience, and self-worth while reducing anxiety, depression, and self-criticism. Writing self-compassion letters is a practical application of this concept, allowing individuals to practice and reinforce compassionate self-talk consciously. This exercise helps in soothing emotional pain and strengthens the capacity for self-kindness in the face of future difficulties.

Section 5: Integrating Self-Awareness into Daily Life

Daily Practices for Self-Reflection

Integrating self-awareness into daily life begins with establishing routines for self-reflection that allow for continued self-discovery and emotional growth. Two powerful tools for fostering this ongoing exploration are journaling and mindfulness practices.

Journaling Prompts: Daily journaling provides a private space to express thoughts, feelings, and experiences. It can help you track your emotional responses and recognize patterns over time. Some prompts to start with could include:

- What emotions did I feel today, and what triggered them?
- In what moments did I feel most aligned with my values?
- How did I respond to challenges today, and what can I learn from these responses?

Mindfulness Practices: Mindfulness involves paying attention to the present moment without judgment. Daily mindfulness practices can range from mindful breathing exercises to engaging fully in everyday activities (like eating or walking) with focused attention. These practices help ground you in the present, enhancing self-awareness and reducing reactivity.

Building Resilience through Self-Awareness

Self-awareness not only aids in understanding oneself but also in building resilience. You can better navigate life's challenges and setbacks by becoming more aware of your thoughts, feelings, and behaviors. Strategies for using self-awareness to foster resilience include:

- **Identifying Personal Strengths and Limitations:** Understanding your strengths allows you to lean on them during difficult times while recognizing your limitations can guide you in seeking support when needed.

- **Setting Boundaries:** Self-awareness helps you recognize when to say no and establish healthy boundaries, protecting your energy and well-being.

- **Adaptive Coping Strategies:** Recognizing how you typically respond to stress enables you to develop more adaptive coping mechanisms, such as seeking social support, practicing relaxation techniques, or reevaluating your perspective on challenges.

- **Embracing Growth Mindset:** Viewing challenges as opportunities for growth rather than insurmountable obstacles can transform how you approach setbacks, leading to greater resilience and adaptability.

Daily Self-Reflection Prompts: Fostering Deeper Self-Awareness

Objective:

This exercise aims to utilize daily self-reflection prompts to cultivate a deeper level of self-awareness and understanding. By engaging with these prompts regularly, you can gain insights into your thoughts, feelings, behaviors, and the underlying patterns that influence your relationships and daily life.

Materials Needed:

- A journal or a digital note-taking app.
- A pen if using a physical journal.

Instructions:

1. **Setup:** Choose a quiet time for reflection, such as morning or evening. Ensure you have a comfortable space to sit and write without interruptions.

2. **Engaging with Prompts:** Each day, select a prompt from the list below or create your own based on what feels most relevant. Spend 5-10 minutes writing your response. Don't censor yourself; let your thoughts and feelings flow freely.

3. **Daily Prompts:**
   - Day 1: What am I grateful for today, and why?
   - Day 2: When did I feel most connected to others today?
   - Day 3: What triggered stress or anxiety for me today, and how did I respond?
   - Day 4: How did I practice self-compassion today?
   - Day 5: What is one thing I learned about myself today?
   - Day 6: How did I contribute to my relationships today?
   - Day 7: What is one change I can make to improve my daily routine?

4. **Reflection:** At the end of each week, review your responses. Look for patterns in your thoughts, feelings, and behaviors. Reflect on any discoveries or insights you've gained about yourself and your interactions with others.

5. **Adjustment and Growth:** Identify personal growth or adjustment areas based on your weekly reflections. Set small, actionable goals for the coming week related to these insights.

Engaging with daily self-reflection prompts is a powerful practice for developing self-awareness and emotional intelligence. It allows you to pause, evaluate, and understand your inner world, leading to meaningful changes in how you relate to yourself and others.

Explanation:

Daily self-reflection prompts are a tool inspired by mindfulness and cognitive-behavioral therapy practices. They encourage introspection, which is crucial for recognizing and understanding our emotional patterns, triggers, and interactions with the world. Regular engagement with these prompts can lead to greater emotional regulation, empathy, and a deeper connection with oneself and others. This exercise is designed to be flexible, allowing you to explore various thoughts and emotions that arise daily, fostering a grounded and centered approach to personal development and relationship building.

Emotion Body Mapping: Identifying Physical Manifestations of Emotions

Objective:

This exercise aims to enhance self-awareness and emotional intelligence by identifying where you physically feel different emotions in the body. By creating an Emotion Body Map, you can visualize and better understand the connection between your emotions and physical sensations, aiding in emotional regulation and mindfulness.

Materials Needed:

- Large paper or a digital drawing app.
- Colored pens, markers, or digital drawing tools.
- A quiet space for reflection and drawing.

Instructions:

1. **Preparation:** Find a comfortable and quiet space to sit or stand to draw. Prepare your large paper or digital app, and select a range of colors for different emotions.

2. **Drawing a Basic Body Outline:** Start by drawing a simple body outline. This doesn't need to be detailed or anatomically perfect; a basic human silhouette will suffice.

3. **Reflection and Emotion Selection:** Reflect on a range of emotions you've experienced recently - joy, sadness, anger, fear, love, surprise, disgust, and any other significant to you. For each emotion, think about where you feel it in the body.

4. **Color Coding and Mapping:** Assign a color to each emotion you've listed. Using those colors, fill in the body outline where you feel each emotion. Use brush strokes, dots, or any shape representing how the emotion manifests.

5. ***Labeling and Noting Sensations:*** Next to each colored area, label the emotion and, if possible, describe the sensation (e.g., "tight," "warm," "tingly"). This helps further to solidify the connection between emotion and physical sensation.

6. ***Reflection and Analysis:*** Once you've completed your map, reflect on what you've created. Consider the following questions: Were there any surprises about where you feel emotions in your body? Are there areas of the body that hold multiple emotions? What might this indicate? How might awareness of these physical sensations serve as cues for managing emotions?

Conclusion:

Emotion Body Mapping is a powerful tool for deepening your understanding of how emotions manifest physically within your body. Regularly engaging in this practice can develop greater emotional awareness and mindfulness, crucial for emotional well-being and self-regulation.

Explanation:

Emotion Body Mapping is based on the concept that emotions are not just mental experiences but also have physical counterparts in the body. This exercise draws on principles from somatic psychology, which emphasizes the interconnectedness of mind and body. Recognizing and understanding these physical sensations associated with emotions can enhance emotional intelligence, providing new strategies for managing emotions effectively. It encourages a holistic approach to emotional health, recognizing the body as an essential component of emotional experience.

Chapter 5
Cultivating Secure Attachment from Within

In the heart of fostering enduring, fulfilling relationships lies the journey toward cultivating secure attachment within ourselves. This quest moves beyond merely understanding the mechanics of anxious attachment—it's about embarking on a transformative path that leads to an inner sanctuary of confidence and emotional security. Secure attachment, characterized by trust, emotional availability, and resilience, starkly contrasts the anxious attachment style, often mired in fear, uncertainty, and a perpetual search for validation.

The essence of secure attachment is not just in the comfort it brings to our relationships but also in the foundation for personal growth and well-being. Unlike anxious attachment, which can leave individuals feeling perpetually on edge, secure attachment fosters a sense of safety that allows for vulnerability, openness, and true connection.

This chapter delves into the principles and practices essential for cultivating such a secure base within oneself. Through a blend of theoretical insights and practical strategies, we aim to guide you from the shores of anxiety and fear to the solid ground of confidence and security in your relationships. You will learn how to navigate the internal landscapes of your emotions, beliefs, and behaviors, transforming them in ways that foster secure attachments in your life.

As we explore these transformative practices, remember that the path to secure attachment is personal and unique. It involves deep self-reflection, a willingness to confront and heal old wounds, and the courage to embrace new ways of relating to oneself and others. This chapter is your guide through that journey, offering a comprehensive overview of cultivating the secure attachment that is the cornerstone of healthy, satisfying relationships.

Cultivating a secure attachment from within is intricate and profoundly rewarding. It requires a commitment to self-discovery, self-compassion, and a willingness to embrace change. This chapter aims to guide you through this transformative journey, illuminating the path from anxious attachment towards a more secure, confident, and fulfilling way of connecting with oneself and others.

The Essence of Secure Attachment vs. Anxious Attachment

To appreciate the significance of cultivating secure attachment qualities, it's essential to understand the core differences between secure and anxious attachment styles. At its heart, secure attachment is characterized by a deep sense of worthiness, emotional resilience, and a balanced perspective on relationships and independence. Individuals with a secure attachment style tend to trust in the stability of their relationships, feel comfortable with closeness and autonomy, and communicate their needs and feelings effectively.

In contrast, anxious attachment often arises from a fear of abandonment and an underlying sense of unworthiness. This fear can lead to hyper-vigilance regarding the state of one's relationships, a tendency to cling to or seek constant reassurance, and difficulties in communicating needs and boundaries in a balanced way. The anxious attachment style is not a life sentence but a pattern formed through past experiences, which means it can be transformed through intentional practice and self-reflection.

The Transformative Power of Internalizing Secure Attachment Qualities

The journey from anxious to secure attachment begins within. It involves a conscious effort to internalize the qualities that define secure attachment: self-worth, trust, resilience, and effective communication. This transformative process is not about becoming someone you're not but rather about rediscovering and reinforcing the inherent strengths and capacities within you.

1. **Self-Worth:** Cultivating a deep-seated belief in your worthiness is the cornerstone of secure attachment. This involves challenging and rewriting the internal narratives that tell you you're not enough unless others validate you. Self-compassion exercises, affirmations, and mindfulness can be powerful tools in reinforcing your sense of worth.

2. **Trust:** Developing trust in yourself and the stability of your relationship is another critical step. This includes learning to trust your ability to handle life's uncertainties

and the resilience of your connections with others, even in the face of disagreements or distance.

3. ***Emotional Resilience:*** Building emotional resilience allows you to navigate the ups and downs of relationships without losing your sense of self or becoming overwhelmed by fear and anxiety. Techniques such as emotional regulation, seeking supportive relationships, and engaging in activities that foster a sense of achievement and joy can enhance resilience.

4. ***Effective Communication:*** Transforming anxious attachment involves learning to communicate your needs, desires, and boundaries in a clear, assertive, and empathetic manner. This means moving away from passive aggression or avoidance patterns and towards open, honest, and direct communication.

By internalizing these qualities, you move towards a more secure attachment style and open up a new realm of possibilities for deeper, more satisfying relationships. This chapter will delve into these areas, providing practical strategies and exercises to guide you toward cultivating secure attachment from within. Let us embark on this journey with openness, courage, and hope for the transformative power of growth and change.

Steps to Internalize the Qualities of Secure Attachment

Cultivating the qualities of secure attachment is a transformative process that enhances our relationships and overall sense of self. Central to this journey is the development of self-reliance and independence, which are pivotal in transitioning from anxious to secure attachment. This section outlines practical steps and exercises designed to foster these qualities, helping you to build confidence in your abilities and decisions.

Building Confidence in One's Abilities and Decisions
Confidence in one's abilities and decisions is a hallmark of secure attachment. It stems from a deep trust in oneself and an understanding that it's okay to make mistakes as part of the learning and growth process. Here's how to start building this confidence:

- ***Reflect on Past Successes:*** Regularly acknowledge and celebrate your achievements, no matter how small. This practice can reinforce your belief in your capabilities.

- ***Make Decisions Independently:*** Start with small decisions, gradually working up to more significant choices. This builds the muscle of trust in your judgment.

- ***Self-Soothing Techniques:*** Develop strategies to calm and reassure yourself when doubts arise. Techniques can include mindfulness, positive self-talk, or engaging in activities that you find soothing and affirming.

Emotional Regulation

Emotional regulation is a cornerstone of secure attachment, allowing individuals to manage their emotional responses in a way that fosters resilience, understanding, and healthy relationships. Effectively managing emotions is not about suppressing feelings but acknowledging them and choosing responses that align with long-term well-being and relationship goals.

Techniques for Effectively Managing Emotions

Mindfulness: This involves staying present with your emotions without judgment. By observing your feelings as they arise, you can gain perspective and reduce the intensity of emotional reactions.

Deep Breathing: A simple yet powerful tool for calming the nervous system. Deep, slow breaths can help reduce anxiety and emotional reactivity, making it easier to approach situations with clarity.

Cognitive Restructuring: This technique involves identifying and challenging negative thought patterns that fuel emotional distress, replacing them with more balanced, constructive thoughts.

Self-Compassion: Practicing kindness and understanding towards oneself during difficult moments can reduce emotional suffering and promote emotional healing.

Case Study: Transforming Impulsive Reactions into Mindful Responses

Maria, a client with a history of anxious attachment, often found herself reacting impulsively during conflicts with her partner, leading to regret and further anxiety. Through therapy,

Maria learned to apply emotional regulation techniques, particularly mindfulness and cognitive restructuring, to manage her reactions.

When faced with potential conflict, Maria practiced pausing before responding, using deep breathing to calm herself. She then engaged in mindfulness, observing her emotions without immediately acting. This pause allowed her to use cognitive restructuring to challenge her initial thoughts of abandonment and reinterpret her partner's actions more generously.

Over time, Maria noticed a significant shift in her relationship dynamics. Her mindful responses led to more constructive conversations, and her partner felt encouraged to be more open and supportive. Maria's journey illustrates the transformative power of emotional regulation in moving from impulsive reactions to mindful, intentional responses.

Practical Exercise: Mindfulness and Cognitive Restructuring. The Pause Practice

Purpose: To integrate mindfulness and cognitive restructuring into daily life, transforming impulsive reactions into thoughtful responses.

Identify a Trigger: Think of a situation that typically triggers an intense emotional reaction. It could be a comment, a specific behavior from someone else, or a particular event.

Plan Your Pause: Decide on a cue reminding you to pause when the trigger occurs. This could be a physical gesture (e.g., placing your hand on your heart), a visual cue, or a short phrase you say to yourself.

Practice Deep Breathing: During the pause, take several deep breaths to help calm your physiological response and give you space to reflect.

Apply Mindfulness: Observe your emotions and thoughts without judgment. Acknowledge them as they are, recognizing that they are temporary and do not control you.

Engage in Cognitive Restructuring: Ask yourself if your initial thoughts about the situation are fully accurate or if there might be another way to view it. Challenge catastrophic thinking and consider more balanced perspectives.

Choose Your Response: Decide how to respond based on reflection rather than immediate emotional impulses.

By regularly practicing this exercise, you can develop greater mastery over your emotional responses, leading to more secure attachment behaviors and healthier relationships. Emotional regulation is a skill that, with practice, can significantly enhance your life and connections with others.

Resilience in the Face of Adversity

Resilience is the capacity to bounce back from setbacks, adapt to change, and keep moving forward in adversity. It's a crucial component of secure attachment, as it enables individuals to maintain a stable sense of self and relationship security, even when faced with challenges. Developing resilience involves a combination of mindset, emotional regulation, and practical strategies to navigate difficult times.

Strategies for Overcoming Setbacks

Acceptance: Recognize that setbacks and challenges are part of life. Accepting them reduces resistance and opens up space for constructive action.

Seek Support: Lean on friends, family, or professionals for support. Sharing your experiences and receiving encouragement can significantly bolster your resilience.

Set Realistic Goals: Break down overwhelming challenges into manageable steps. Achieving small goals can boost your confidence and motivation to tackle bigger issues.

Focus on What You Can Control: Concentrate your energy on aspects of your situation that you can influence rather than what is beyond your control.

Practice Self-Care: Regularly engage in activities that promote physical, emotional, and mental well-being to maintain your strength during tough times.

Success Story: Embracing Optimism to Navigate Challenges

James, who had struggled with an anxious attachment style, faced a series of professional setbacks that left him feeling defeated and insecure in his relationships. However, instead of succumbing to despair, James focused on cultivating optimism and resilience. He began by setting small, daily goals to rebuild his confidence, seeking support from a therapist and trusted friends, and dedicating each day to self-care activities he enjoyed, such as reading and walking in nature.

Over time, James's optimistic outlook helped him view challenges as opportunities for growth rather than insurmountable obstacles. This shift in perspective helped him navigate his professional setbacks more effectively and strengthened his relationships as he became more emotionally available and supportive, reflecting his inner state of resilience.

Exercise: The Gratitude and Growth Journal

Purpose: To cultivate resilience by focusing on gratitude and growth opportunities in the face of adversity.

Daily Gratitude: Write down three things you are grateful for each morning or evening. These can be as simple as a sunny day, a supportive conversation with a friend, or a personal achievement. Focusing on gratitude can shift your perspective from what's lacking to what's abundant in your life.

Growth Opportunities: Reflect on a recent challenge or setback and write about it from a growth mindset.

Ask yourself:
- What can I learn from this situation?
- How has this challenge helped me grow?
- What strengths did I discover in myself as a result?

Positive Affirmations: End each journaling session with a positive affirmation that reinforces your ability to overcome difficulties.

For example, "I am resilient and capable of handling life's challenges with grace and strength."

Regular practice of this exercise can enhance your resilience, helping you maintain a positive outlook and secure sense of self, even in the face of adversity. By embracing optimism and focusing on growth, you lay the foundation for a resilient, secure attachment style that can weather any storm.

Techniques for Reprogramming Old Beliefs and Patterns

Transforming old beliefs and patterns, particularly those contributing to anxious attachment, requires a conscious, systematic approach. The goal is to identify, challenge, and replace negative beliefs with more adaptive, positive ones. This process fosters a journey towards secure attachment by encouraging a more compassionate and realistic view of oneself and one's relationships.

Identifying and Challenging Negative Beliefs

1. ***Awareness:*** The first step is to become aware of your negative beliefs. These often manifest as automatic thoughts in response to certain triggers or situations.

2. ***Examination:*** Once identified, examine these beliefs critically. Ask yourself, "Is this thought based on facts or assumptions? Is it a helpful way of viewing the situation?"

3. ***Challenge:*** Challenge these beliefs by looking for evidence that contradicts them. Consider alternative explanations and perspectives that are more balanced and compassionate.

Anecdotes: Stories of Changing Attachment Patterns

Case 1: Jamie's Journey

Jamie grew up in a household where emotional expression was discouraged, leading to beliefs that showing vulnerability was a sign of weakness. This belief system manifested in an anxious attachment style characterized by difficulty trusting others and expressing emotions in relationships. Through therapy, Jamie learned to identify and challenge these deep-seated beliefs. By reflecting on experiences where vulnerability led to stronger connections rather than rejection, Jamie gradually embraced emotional expression as a strength, fostering more secure attachments.

Case 2: Alex's Transformation

Alex's history of unstable relationships contributed to a core belief that they were unworthy of love, driving anxious behaviors in romantic settings. Through cognitive-behavioral techniques, Alex began to identify instances where this belief was proven wrong—times when they were loved and appreciated for who they were. By focusing on these instances and practicing affirmations of self-worth, Alex started to break the cycle of anxious attachment, moving towards healthier, more secure relationship dynamics.

Exercise: Rewriting Your Attachment Narrative

Purpose: To use cognitive-behavioral strategies, affirmations, and visualization to reprogram old beliefs and patterns related to attachment.

1. *Identify and Write Down Negative Beliefs*: Reflect on beliefs that contribute to your anxious attachment style. For example, "I am not worthy of love" or "If I show my true self, I will be rejected."

2. *Challenge These Beliefs:* Write down evidence that contradicts these beliefs. Include past experiences, qualities you possess, and positive feedback from others.

3. *Develop New Affirmations:* Based on your reflections, create positive affirmations that reinforce secure attachment beliefs. For instance, "I am worthy of love and respect," or "My vulnerability is a strength that fosters deeper connections."

4. *Visualization:* Close your eyes and visualize a scenario where you embody these new beliefs. Imagine yourself in a relationship scenario where you act out of security rather than anxiety—expressing needs openly, responding calmly to conflict, and enjoying mutual trust and respect.

5. *Daily Practice:* Dedicate a few minutes each day to repeat your affirmations and engage in visualization. Over time, this practice can help solidify these new, positive beliefs and patterns in your subconscious, aiding the transition toward more secure attachment.

Reprogramming old beliefs and patterns is a journey that requires patience and persistence. By applying these techniques, you can gradually shift your attachment style towards one that is more secure, fostering healthier and more fulfilling relationships.

Fostering Secure Attachment Skills (SAS)

Practical Exercises for Everyday Life

Cultivating secure attachment skills (SAS) is an ongoing process that enhances our ability to form and maintain healthy, fulfilling relationships. Integrating practical exercises into our daily routines can significantly impact our attachment style, steering us towards more secure patterns of relating to ourselves and others. This section outlines daily practices designed to foster secure attachment behaviors, strengthening the foundations of trust, empathy, and emotional resilience.

Daily Reflection: Begin each day with a moment of reflection. Consider your intentions for the day in terms of relating to others. Set goals to practice active listening, empathy, and openness in your interactions. Reflection helps set a positive tone for the day, focusing on growth and connection.

Mindfulness Meditation: Incorporate mindfulness meditation into your daily routine to enhance present-moment awareness and emotional regulation. Mindfulness fosters a non-judgmental stance towards your thoughts and feelings, which is crucial for developing secure attachment by reducing reactivity and promoting understanding.

Gratitude Journaling: Keeping a gratitude journal can shift the focus from what's lacking to what's abundant in your relationships and life. Regularly jotting down things you're grateful for can enhance positive emotions, improve self-esteem, and strengthen bonds with others.

Effective Communication Practice: Make a conscious effort to practice effective communication techniques daily. This includes expressing your needs and feelings clearly and respectfully, active listening, and assertive yet compassionate dialogue. Effective communication is key to building and maintaining secure attachments.

Boundary Setting: Secure attachment involves understanding and respecting personal boundaries—yours and others. Daily, reflect on your boundaries and communicate them as needed. This practice builds respect, trust, and mutual understanding in relationships.

Emotional Check-ins: Several times daily, pause to check in with your emotions. Identifying and acknowledging your feelings as they arise can help you understand your emotional triggers and patterns, leading to better emotional regulation and secure attachment behaviors.

Connection Rituals: Establish daily rituals to connect with loved ones, whether it's a morning text, an evening walk, or a nightly chat before bed. These rituals reinforce the stability and predictability essential for secure attachment.

Exercise: The Emotional Safety Dialogue

Purpose: To enhance emotional safety in relationships through effective communication practices.

Set Aside Time: Schedule a regular time with your partner dedicated to discussing your relationship openly and honestly, without distractions.

Use "I" Statements: When expressing your thoughts and feelings, use "I" statements to own your emotions and avoid placing blame.

- For example, "I feel worried when we don't talk about our plans," instead of "You never tell me what's happening."

Practice Active Listening: When your partner is speaking, give them your full attention. Listen to understand, not to respond. Reflect on what you've heard to ensure you've understood correctly.

Validate Each Other's Feelings: Acknowledge your partner's feelings, even if you have a different perspective. Validation can be as simple as saying, "I see why you feel that way," or "It makes sense to me that you'd feel upset about that."

Seek to Understand, Then to Be Understood: Ask questions to deepen your understanding of your partner's perspective before offering your viewpoint. This fosters a deeper connection and ensures both partners feel heard and understood.

By regularly practicing these communication techniques, couples can enhance the emotional safety of their relationship, creating a secure base from which both partners can thrive. This exercise strengthens the relationship foundation and promotes individual growth and secure attachment within the partnership.

Using Affirmations to Reinforce Secure Attachment Qualities

Positive affirmations are short, powerful statements that, when repeated frequently, can alter our beliefs, thoughts, and behaviors. To reinforce secure attachment qualities, affirmations should focus on trust, self-worth, and the ability to form healthy relationships.

Examples of affirmations include:
1. "I am worthy of love and respect from both myself and others."
2. I trust in my ability to navigate the ups and downs of relationships."
3. "I can give and receive love freely and openly."
4. "I embrace vulnerability as a strength, not a weakness."
5. "My relationships are based on mutual respect and understanding."

The key to effective affirmations is consistency and belief in spoken words. Affirmations should be repeated daily, preferably in the morning and before bedtime, to maximize their impact on the subconscious mind.

Chapter Exercises

Secure Attachment Visualization Exercise Manual

Objective:

This exercise aims to foster a sense of secure attachment within individuals by utilizing the power of guided imagery. By envisioning a secure version of themselves in relationships, participants can start internalizing feelings of safety, trust, and balance, characteristic of secure attachment styles.

Introduction to Guided Imagery:

Guided imagery is a relaxation technique that involves focusing the mind on peaceful, detailed images. This practice can help reduce anxiety, improve mood, and foster a deeper sense of security and confidence within interpersonal relationships.

Preparing for the Exercise:

Find a Quiet Space: Choose a comfortable, quiet place where you won't be disturbed.

Adopt a Comfortable Position: Sit or lie comfortably. Use cushions or blankets as needed.

Set an Intention: Set an intention for this exercise before you begin. For example, "I am cultivating a sense of security and trust within myself."

Step-by-Step Guide:

- *Relaxation:* Begin by taking deep, slow breaths. Inhale deeply through your nose, filling your lungs completely, and exhale slowly through your mouth. With each breath, allow any tension in your body to melt away. Continue this breathing pattern for a few minutes until you feel relaxed.

- *Envision Your Secure Self:* Imagine a version of yourself who feels completely secure in relationships. This is a version of you that trusts easily, communicates openly, and maintains healthy boundaries. Picture yourself standing with a posture that reflects confidence and openness.

- *Imagine a Supportive Environment:* Visualize yourself surrounded by a supportive environment. This could be a warm, inviting space where you feel safe and loved. Notice the colors, textures, and objects that make this space comforting.

- *Interact with a Loved One:* In your mind's eye, imagine interacting with a partner, friend, or family member. Envision a scenario where you are expressing your needs clearly and calmly. See the other person responding with understanding and empathy. Focus on the feelings of trust and connection that arise.

- *Handle a Conflict:* Now, imagine a situation where a conflict arises. See yourself handling this conflict with maturity and calmness, actively listening, and seeking a solution that benefits both parties. Notice how secure and grounded you feel, even in disagreement.

- *Reflect on Your Feelings:* Pay attention to the emotions you are experiencing during these visualizations. Do you feel a sense of calm? Trust? Love? Acknowledge these feelings and remind yourself that they are within your reach.

- *Reaffirm Your Secure Self:* Conclude the visualization with a positive affirmation about your ability to build and maintain secure attachments. For example, "I can create loving, trusting relationships."

Example Scenario:

Imagine you're planning a weekend getaway with your partner. In the past, you might have felt anxious about expressing your preferences or worried about the trip not being perfect. However, in this visualization, see yourself confidently discussing plans with your partner, expressing what you'd like to do, and being open to their suggestions. Visualize both of you coming to a happy compromise, feeling excited about the trip, and appreciating the ease of communication.

Conclusion:

Take a few deep breaths and gently bring your awareness back to the present moment. Open your eyes when you're ready. Reflect on the experience, noting any insights or feelings that emerged. Remember, the goal of this exercise is not to achieve perfection but to practice envisioning yourself in a secure attachment state.

Post-Exercise Reflection:

After completing the visualization, it might be helpful to journal about your experience. Consider the following questions:

- What did it feel like to envision yourself as securely attached?
- Were there any moments that felt particularly challenging or enlightening?
- How can you incorporate the feelings or insights gained from this exercise into your daily life?

Practice Regularly:

Like any skill, cultivating a sense of secure attachment through visualization takes practice. Aim to perform this exercise regularly, whether daily or weekly, to reinforce the feelings of security, trust, and balance in your relationships.

Self-Reliance Challenges Exercise Manual

Objective:

The objective of these self-reliance challenges is to incrementally build confidence and autonomy. By setting and achieving small, manageable goals, individuals can strengthen their belief in their abilities, enhancing their self-reliance and independence.

Introduction:

Self-reliance is the ability to trust and depend on one's own capabilities in managing life's challenges. It involves making decisions, solving problems, and feeling confident in taking care of yourself. This exercise manual provides a structured approach to developing self-reliance through small, achievable challenges.

Preparing for the Challenges:

- *Assess Your Current Self-Reliance:* Reflect on areas where you feel dependent on others or lack confidence in your abilities.
- *Set Clear, Achievable Goals:* Identify specific, small challenges that can help you build confidence in these areas.
- *Create a Supportive Environment:* Although the focus is on self-reliance, having a supportive network can provide encouragement and feedback.

Step-by-Step Guide:

Challenge 1: Daily Decision-Making:
Objective: Improve confidence in making daily decisions independently.

Example: For one week, make all minor decisions (e.g., what to eat, wear, or watch) without seeking others' opinions.

Reflection: At the end of the week, reflect on how making these decisions made you feel. Did you notice a change in your confidence levels?

Challenge 2: Problem-Solving:
Objective: Enhance problem-solving skills by tackling small problems on your own.

Example: Identify a small problem you're facing (e.g., a malfunctioning appliance or a scheduling conflict) and resolve it independently.

Reflection: Consider the steps you took to resolve the problem. How did it feel to find a solution on your own?

Challenge 3: Learning a New Skill:
Objective: Build confidence by learning a new skill independently.

Example: Choose a new skill relevant to your interests or needs (e.g., cooking a new recipe, basic car maintenance) and learn it through online resources or books.

Reflection: Reflect on the learning process. How has mastering a new skill impacted your self-view?

Challenge 4: Financial Independence:
Objective: Increase financial self-reliance by managing a small budget.

Example: Set a budget for a week or a month for a particular aspect of your spending (e.g., groceries, entertainment) and stick to it strictly.

Reflection: Analyze your spending behavior and the choices you made. How did managing your budget independently affect your sense of self-reliance?

Challenge 5: Social Independence:
Objective: Improve confidence in social settings without relying on others.

Example: Attend a social event or a class where you don't know anyone. Focus on initiating at least one conversation.

Reflection: Reflect on the experience of navigating a social setting independently. What did you learn about yourself?

Conclusion:
After completing these challenges, reflect on your journey towards self-reliance. Acknowledge your growth and the areas where you've become more confident and independent. Self-reliance is a continuous journey, and every small step is progress.

Post-Exercise Reflection:
- What challenges were most beneficial for you? Why?
- In which areas do you feel more confident and independent?
- How can you continue to build on this foundation of self-reliance?

Practice Regularly:
Self-reliance is built through consistent practice and stepping out of your comfort zone. Continue to set new challenges for yourself, gradually increasing their difficulty as you grow more confident in your abilities.

Resilience Building Activities Exercise Manual

Objective:

This manual is designed to guide you through resilience-building activities that focus on identifying past adversities you've overcome and the strengths you used during those times. Applying these insights to current challenges can enhance your resilience, enabling you to better navigate life's ups and downs.

Introduction to Resilience:

Resilience is the ability to bounce back from setbacks, adapt to change, and persevere in adversity. It involves behaviors, thoughts, and actions that can be developed and strengthened over time.

Preparing for the Activities:

1. Reflect on Past Experiences: Consider past situations where you faced challenges, setbacks, or adversities.

2. Identify Your Strengths: Consider the strengths and qualities that helped you overcome those challenges.

3. Set a Positive Mindset: Approach these activities with an open mind and a willingness to learn and grow.

Core Activities for Building Resilience:

Resilience Reflection:
Purpose: Reflect on past adversities and identify the strengths used to overcome them.

How to Do It: Write down three challenging situations you've faced. For each situation, identify the strengths and skills you employed to overcome the adversity. Reflect on how these experiences have contributed to your growth.

Example: If you overcame a difficult job loss by networking and learning new skills, you demonstrated adaptability, perseverance, and a willingness to learn.

Gratitude Journaling:

Purpose: Cultivate a sense of gratitude for your strengths and past experiences.

How to Do It: Keep a daily gratitude journal where you note three things you are grateful for daily, focusing on personal strengths and past successes.

Example: Express gratitude for your resilience in navigating a health scare, highlighting your optimism and support network.

Strengths Mapping:

Purpose: Visually map out your strengths and how they can be applied to current challenges.

How to Do It: Create a strengths map by listing your key strengths and drawing connections to how each one can help you manage current life challenges.

Example: Link your strength in problem-solving to managing work-related stress, illustrating specific strategies you can use.

Solution-Focused Thinking:

Purpose: Develop a solution-focused approach to current challenges.

How to Do It: Choose a challenge and brainstorm possible solutions, focusing on actionable steps that leverage your strengths.

Example: If you're facing relationship difficulties, use your communication skills and empathy to devise a plan for improving understanding and connection.

Resilience Action Plan:

Purpose: Create a detailed plan to overcome a challenge using your strengths.

How to Do It: Select one current challenge and develop an action plan that outlines specific steps, resources needed, and how your strengths will be utilized.

Example: If you're working on a challenging project, plan steps for completing the project, including time management strategies and seeking feedback, highlighting your organization and persistence.

Conclusion:

Resilience is not a trait you have or don't have; it involves learning and growth. By reflecting on past adversities and recognizing the strengths that helped you overcome them, you can apply these insights to current and future challenges, building a stronger, more resilient self.

Practice Regularly:

Regularly engaging in these resilience-building activities can help you strengthen your ability to cope with stress and adversity. Reflect on your progress, and remember that building resilience is a journey that involves continuous effort and commitment.

Reprogramming Negative Beliefs Exercise Manual

Objective:

This manual aims to guide individuals through identifying and challenging negative beliefs about themselves and their relationships. Addressing these beliefs head-on can reshape your thoughts towards more positive and empowering ones.

Introduction:

Negative beliefs about ourselves and our capabilities can significantly impact our mental health, relationships, and overall well-being. This manual introduces exercises based on Cognitive Behavioral Therapy (CBT) principles to help you identify, challenge, and reprogram these negative beliefs.

1. Identifying Negative Core Beliefs:

Begin by identifying your negative core beliefs, especially those that impact your view of yourself and your interactions with others. Consider areas of your life where you feel most vulnerable or insecure.

- To familiarize yourself with examples, perform an internet search on 'core beliefs'.
- Reflect on your anxiety around social situations or personal insecurities.
- Write down one negative core belief you've identified and consider where it might have originated.

2. Challenging Negative Beliefs:

After identifying your negative core belief, challenge it by questioning its validity and looking for evidence that contradicts it.

- *Ask yourself:* What evidence do I have that supports or contradicts this belief?
- Consider alternative explanations or perspectives.
- Write down a more balanced or positive belief that reflects a more accurate view of yourself or the situation.

3. Practice Active Listening in Social Situations:

Active listening can help shift focus from your internal negative beliefs to the external world, improving social interactions and confidence.

- Focus on truly hearing and understanding what others are saying rather than planning your response or worrying about being judged.
- Notice how being present and engaging in conversations can challenge negative assumptions about social interactions.

Conclusion:

Reprogramming negative beliefs is a process that requires time, patience, and practice. Regularly engaging in these exercises can gradually shift your thought patterns towards more positive and empowering ones, improving your mental health and relationships.

Positive Affirmation Practice Exercise Manual

Objective:

This manual guides individuals in developing and practicing daily affirmations to foster secure attachment and enhance self-worth. Through consistent affirmation practice, you can cultivate a more positive self-image and improve your relationships.

Introduction to Positive Affirmations:

Positive affirmations are short, powerful statements that, when spoken or thought repeatedly, can influence your subconscious mind, helping to reshape your thoughts, beliefs, and attitudes towards a more positive perspective. This practice is particularly beneficial for reinforcing feelings of secure attachment and boosting self-worth.

Preparing for Affirmation Practice:

1. Choose a Quiet, Comfortable Space: Select a place where you can be alone and undisturbed during your practice.

2. Set a Regular Time: Dedicate a specific time each day for your affirmation practice to develop a routine.

3. Mindset for Success: Approach your practice with an open heart and mind, believing in the power of your words.

Steps to Develop Your Positive Affirmations:

1. Reflect on Your Needs: Identify areas related to attachment and self-worth where you seek improvement or support. Example: If you often feel unworthy of love, you might focus on affirmations reinforcing your inherent value.

2. Craft Your Affirmations: Write affirmations in the present tense as if you already embody or experience the positive state. Be specific and positive in your wording.

- Example: "I deserve love and form secure, healthy relationships."

3. Incorporate Emotion: Affirmations are most effective when they evoke a positive emotional response. Try to feel the truth of your affirmation as you say it.

- Example: When reciting an affirmation about self-worth, envision yourself radiating confidence and being respected by others.

Daily Affirmation Practice:

1. Morning Kick-Start: Begin your day by reciting secure attachment and self-worth affirmations.

- Example: "I am confident in my ability to express my needs in relationships."

2. Midday Boost: Take a few moments in the middle of your day to reaffirm your positive statements. This can be a quick mental recitation to reinforce the morning's practice.

3. Evening Reflection: End your day by reflecting on moments where you felt your affirmations were challenged or confirmed. Reaffirm your positive statements with any adjustments based on your reflections.

Examples of Positive Affirmations for Secure Attachment and Self-Worth:

- I am worthy of receiving love and kindness from myself and others.
- I trust my ability to create and maintain healthy relationships.
- I embrace my strengths and weaknesses equally in my journey towards personal growth.
- I am secure in my identity and my value in my relationships.

Conclusion:

Positive affirmation practice is a powerful tool for transforming your inner dialogue, enhancing feelings of secure attachment, and boosting self-worth. Consistency is key to seeing results, so integrate this practice into your daily routine and witness the positive changes in your mindset and relationships.

Practice Regularly:

Commit to your affirmation practice daily. Over time, you will notice a shift in your thoughts and beliefs towards a more positive and secure attachment with yourself and in your relationships. Remember, the transformation begins with your willingness to believe in the power of your affirmations.

Chapter 6

Understanding Conflict in the Context of Anxious Attachment

Conflict is an inevitable aspect of any relationship, a truth that holds regardless of the strength or duration of the bond between partners. It's essential to begin by normalizing conflict, recognizing it not as a failure or setback but as a natural and, potentially, a constructive part of relational dynamics. The goal, then, is not to avoid conflict altogether—a pursuit that is not only futile but can also suppress genuine expression and lead to resentment—but to develop the skills necessary to handle conflict constructively. This approach transforms conflict from a source of dread to an opportunity for growth, deepening understanding, and fostering intimacy.

For individuals with anxious attachment styles, conflict takes on a particularly poignant and often distressing dimension. The core of anxious attachment is a deep fear of abandonment or rejection, a worry that conflicts, however minor, could precipitate the end of the relationship or lead to significant disapproval from their partner. This fear can lead to behaviors that either escalate the conflict (through attempts to seek reassurance) or avoid it entirely (by suppressing one's own needs and feelings). Neither approach is conducive to healthy, long-term relationship dynamics.

Understanding conflict through the lens of anxious attachment involves recognizing these fears not as overreactions or irrational but as deeply felt concerns that stem from past experiences and internalized beliefs about self-worth and loveability. It's critical, therefore, to approach conflict resolution with a strategy that addresses the immediate disagreement and speaks to these underlying fears, providing a sense of security and reassurance even amid disagreement.

Developing healthy conflict resolution skills is thus doubly important for those with anxious attachment. It's about learning to communicate needs and feelings effectively, but it's also about rewriting the internal script that says conflict threatens love and belonging.

This involves cultivating a mindset that sees conflict as an opportunity to strengthen the relationship, understand and be understood more deeply, and build a foundation of trust that can withstand the inevitable challenges of sharing a life with someone.

In the following sections, we will explore specific strategies and steps to navigate conflict constructively, tailored to the needs and experiences of those with anxious attachment. The aim is to equip you with the tools to survive conflict and use it as a stepping stone toward a more secure, intimate, and fulfilling relationship.

Step-by-Step Blueprint for Constructive Conflict Resolution

Step 1: Self-Regulation Before Engagement

Recognize Emotional Activation: The first step in navigating conflict, especially for those with anxious attachment, is recognizing the signs of emotional activation. This might manifest as a racing heart, a sense of defensiveness, an urge to immediately seek reassurance, or even an impulse to withdraw completely. These physical and emotional cues are your body's way of signaling that you're entering a state of heightened arousal, which is not conducive to constructive dialogue.

When you notice these signs, it's crucial to pause and engage in self-regulation techniques. Breathing exercises can be particularly effective here; for example, the "4-7-8" technique (inhale for 4 seconds, hold for 7, exhale for 8) is a simple method to quickly calm the nervous system. Alternatively, taking a brief timeout—stepping away from the situation to cool down—can help prevent the kind of reactive responses that escalate conflict.

Self-Reflection: Once you've managed to soothe your immediate physiological and emotional reactions, the next step is to engage in a brief period of self-reflection. This involves asking yourself a few key questions to understand what's truly at the heart of the conflict. What specifically triggered your emotional response? Is there a deeper fear or need that this conflict is touching upon, such as a fear of losing your partner or a need for more validation?

This step is not about crafting your argument or planning what to say to win the conflict; it's about understanding your feelings and needs. By clarifying what you're reacting to, you can shift from a defensive or accusatory stance to one that's more open and vulnerable, which is far more conducive to constructive resolution.

Self-reflection also involves recognizing your role in the conflict. Are there ways your behaviors or reactions might have contributed to the escalation? This isn't about self-blame but about taking responsibility for your part, which empowers you to make changes and communicate more effectively.

These initial steps set the stage for a resolution process grounded in self-awareness and mutual respect. By starting with self-regulation and self-reflection, individuals with anxious attachment can better manage their fears and approach conflict not as a threat but as an opportunity for growth and deeper connection.

Step 2: Initiate the Conversation with a Soft Start-Up

Soft Start-Up: After you've taken the time to self-regulate and reflect on your feelings and needs, the next step is to initiate the conversation to minimize defensiveness and open the door for constructive dialogue. This is where the concept of a "soft start-up" comes into play. A soft start-up involves approaching the conversation with gentleness and care, which is especially important for those with anxious attachment who might fear initiating conflict could lead to rejection or abandonment.

To employ a soft start-up, use "I" statements that focus on your feelings and experiences rather than the other person's perceived faults or actions. For example, saying, "I feel upset when we don't spend quality time together," centers your feelings and invites empathy, whereas "You never spend time with me" can be accusatory and may provoke a defensive response. The goal here is to communicate your perspective without implying blame, which can help your partner stay open to hearing your concerns.

Express Needs Clearly: Along with expressing how you feel, it's equally important to clearly articulate your needs and desires. This does not mean demanding your partner change their behavior on the spot but rather expressing what you need positively and constructively. For example, after stating how you feel, you might continue, " I value our time together, and it's important for me to feel connected. Could we look at finding more ways to spend quality time together?"

Expressing your needs clearly from the outset sets a constructive tone for the conversation. It moves the dialogue from a focus on problems to a focus on solutions and shared goals. This step is crucial for creating a space where both partners feel heard and respected and where conflicts are seen not as battles to be won but as opportunities to understand each other better and strengthen the relationship.

For individuals with anxious attachment, this step is particularly powerful. It directly addresses the fear of not being valued or heard within the relationship by actively engaging in behaviors that seek mutual understanding and closeness. By initiating the conversation with a soft start-up and clear expression of needs, you're advocating for your emotional well-being and inviting your partner into a collaborative process of growth and connection.

Step 3: Active Listening and Validation

After initiating the conversation with a soft start-up and clearly expressing your needs, the next crucial step involves active listening and validation. This stage is essential for creating a safe and respectful environment where both partners feel heard and understood, which is especially significant for those with anxious attachment, who may have deep-seated fears of being dismissed or misunderstood.

Active Listening: Active listening is a skill that requires full engagement with your partner's words, emotions, and underlying needs. It involves more than just hearing the words; it's about understanding the message and emotions behind them. Here are some techniques to enhance active listening:

Maintain Eye Contact: Eye contact conveys that you fully focus on your partner and value what they say. It's a non-verbal way of showing respect and attention.

Nodding and Other Non-verbal Cues: Nodding your head and other affirming gestures signals that you follow along and engage in the conversation. These cues encourage your partner to continue sharing.

Summarizing and Paraphrasing: After your partner has finished speaking, summarize or paraphrase what they've said to ensure you've understood correctly. For instance, "So, I'm hearing that you feel overwhelmed when the house is cluttered, making it hard for you to relax. Is that right?" This not only shows that you are listening but also that you are making an effort to understand their perspective.

Validation: Validation is recognizing and accepting your partner's feelings and perspectives as valid and important, regardless of whether you agree with them. Validation is a powerful tool for building empathy and deepening connection, as it communicates to your partner that their feelings matter to you. Here are some ways to validate your partner:

Acknowledge Their Feelings: Start by acknowledging what your partner is feeling, even if you see the situation differently. For example, "I understand why you felt that way" or "It makes sense to me that you're upset about this."

Express Empathy: Showing empathy doesn't mean you have to agree with everything your partner says; rather, it's about sharing in their emotional experience. Phrases like, "I can see how that situation could be really frustrating," convey empathy and understanding.

Avoid Minimizing or Dismissing: Avoid dismissing or minimizing your partner's feelings, even unintentionally. Comments like, "It's not that big of a deal," can feel invalidating. Instead, focus on understanding and acknowledging their experience.

For individuals with anxious attachment, practicing active listening and validation can be transformative. These skills improve communication and help to counteract fears of abandonment and rejection by reinforcing the bond of trust and mutual respect in the relationship. Through active listening and validation, conflicts become opportunities for growth and deepening intimacy rather than sources of anxiety and disconnection.

Step 4: Focus on the Issue, Not the Person

Navigating conflict constructively requires a careful approach to how problems are addressed. For individuals, especially those with anxious attachment, the manner in which issues are discussed can significantly impact feelings of security and connection in the relationship. This step is about depersonalizing conflict and focusing on the issue at hand, which helps maintain a productive dialogue and reduces the likelihood of defensiveness escalating the conflict.

Depersonalize Conflict: Keeping the conversation focused on the behavior or situation causing concern is crucial, rather than attributing negative intentions or characteristics to your partner. This distinction helps to keep the conversation constructive, as it separates the problem from the person.

- ***For instance,*** instead of saying, "You don't care about our plans," try framing the issue as, "When our plans change at the last minute, I feel disregarded."

This approach communicates your feelings and the situation's impact without casting your partner in a negative light.

Use Specific Examples: To effectively communicate about issues, it's important to use specific, recent examples rather than vague or generalized statements.

Generalizations like "you always" or "you never" can feel overwhelming and unfair, leading to defensiveness rather than understanding. Instead, pinpointing a specific instance provides a concrete basis for the discussion, making it easier to address the problem.

- ***For example,*** "Yesterday, when the dinner plans were canceled, I felt hurt because I was looking forward to spending time together," directly addresses a particular incident, allowing for a more focused and fair conversation.

Focusing on the issue rather than the person also involves recognizing that both partners are navigating their feelings and perspectives. Remember, the goal of conflict resolution isn't to "win" or to prove the other person wrong but to find a mutual understanding and come to a resolution that respects both partners' needs and feelings. By depersonalizing the conflict and using specific examples, you create a foundation for dialogue that is more likely to lead to understanding, compromise, and growth.

This approach facilitates more effective communication and reinforces the security of the relationship for those with anxious attachment. It demonstrates that conflicts can be navigated in a way that respects both individuals' feelings and needs, thereby reducing the fear of conflict leading to abandonment or a breakdown in the relationship.

Step 5: Seek Common Ground and Compromise

The final step in the blueprint for constructive conflict resolution focuses on the forward movement toward resolution. For those with anxious attachment, finding common ground and engaging in compromise is particularly vital, as it reinforces the stability and security of the relationship.

This step transcends the immediate conflict to foster a deeper connection and understanding between partners.

Identifying Shared Goals: At the heart of most conflicts lie opportunities to reaffirm the shared goals, values, and desires that brought you and your partner together.

Even in disagreement, there's common ground in the overarching objectives you share for the relationship, such as mutual respect, love, understanding, or personal growth. Begin negotiations by highlighting these shared aspirations.

- ***For instance, you might say,*** "I know we both value our time together and want to feel connected. How can we address our current challenge in a way that honors that goal?"

Focusing on shared goals shifts the conversation from opposing positions to collaborative problem-solving. It reminds both partners that, despite the conflict, you are ultimately on the same team, working towards the same ends.

Compromise: The art of compromise is crucial in any relationship, especially for those navigating the complexities of anxious attachment. Compromise does not mean one partner always has to give in, or your needs are less important than your partner's. Instead, it's about finding a middle ground where both partners' needs and concerns are acknowledged and addressed.

Discussing compromise involves exploring flexible solutions and being open to alternative outcomes that satisfy both parties. It means sometimes prioritizing the relationship's well-being over individual preferences without completely sacrificing your needs.

- ***For example,*** suppose the conflict revolves around how much time to spend together versus apart. In that case, a compromise might involve agreeing on specific days for quality time together while respecting individual time for personal activities or solitude.

Compromise can be profoundly rewarding, as it often leads to outcomes neither partner could have achieved alone. It strengthens the relationship by demonstrating mutual respect, understanding, and willingness to work together towards a solution that considers both partners' perspectives.

For individuals with anxious attachment, the ability to successfully navigate through to compromise can significantly boost relationship security. It provides tangible evidence that conflicts can be resolved in a way that honors both partners' needs, reinforcing the trust and bond between them. Engaging in this step with empathy, openness, and a willingness to see the other's point of view not only resolves the immediate conflict but also builds a stronger, more resilient foundation for future challenges.

Step 6: Establish Agreements and Future Strategies

Moving from compromise to action, the final cornerstone of constructive conflict resolution involves establishing concrete agreements and devising future strategies. This step is crucial for ensuring the conflict does not become a recurring issue, especially for individuals with anxious attachment, who can greatly benefit from the reassurance and clarity that concrete plans and strategies provide.

Concrete Agreements: Once a compromise is reached, it's important to translate the conceptual understanding into concrete, actionable agreements. These agreements should directly address the root causes of the conflict and outline specific steps both partners commit to taking.

- *For example,* if the compromise involves balancing quality time together with personal time, an agreement might specify setting aside certain nights for date nights and other evenings for individual activities.

The key is specificity—knowing exactly what each person agrees to do differently helps prevent misunderstandings and provides a clear path forward.

Creating concrete agreements also involves setting timelines and, in some cases, establishing how progress will be monitored or discussed. This level of detail ensures that both partners are on the same page and have a shared understanding of what success looks like.

Future Strategies: Beyond resolving the immediate conflict, there's a valuable opportunity to learn from the experience and apply these insights to future disagreements.

Encourage couples to reflect on the conflict resolution process—what worked well, what didn't, and how both partners can better handle similar situations.

Developing future strategies might involve agreeing on a 'signal' for when one partner needs to take a break and self-regulate before continuing a difficult conversation, or it might include a commitment to initiating discussions with a soft start-up to prevent defensiveness from the outset. The goal is to turn the current conflict into a learning opportunity that strengthens the relationship's resilience and the partners' conflict resolution skills.

For individuals with anxious attachment, establishing agreements and future strategies can significantly reduce anxiety around conflicts, knowing there's a plan in place for navigating disagreements constructively. It reinforces the security of the relationship and the commitment of both partners to work through challenges together. This proactive approach resolves the current issue and contributes to a foundation of trust, understanding, and mutual respect that will benefit the relationship in the long term.

Real-World Examples and Role-Plays

Integrating real-world examples and role-play scenarios can significantly enhance understanding and application of the conflict resolution steps discussed. These practical tools allow individuals and couples, especially those with anxious attachment, to visualize and practice the principles in a concrete, hands-on way, bridging the gap between theory and practice.

Real-World Example
Scenario: Alex and Jordan, who have been together for two years, frequently argue about household chores. Alex, who has an anxious attachment style, feels overwhelmed and unsupported when noticing chores are not evenly distributed, fearing that Jordan does not value their shared home or partnership. On the other hand, Jordan feels criticized and underappreciated, leading to defensiveness.

Using the Steps:
- *Step 1 (Self-Regulation and Self-Reflection):* Alex takes a moment to breathe and reflect before initiating the conversation, recognizing the core issue is feeling unsupported, not the chores themselves.

- *Step 2 (Soft Start-Up):* Alex begins the conversation with, "I feel overwhelmed when I see many chores piling up. It makes me feel like we're not working as a team."

- **Step 3 (Active Listening and Validation):** Jordan listens without interrupting, then responds, "I understand you're feeling overwhelmed, and it's not fair to you. Let's figure out how we can divide things more evenly."

- **Step 4 (Focus on the Issue, Not the Person):** They discuss specific tasks and avoid blaming, focusing on how the distribution of chores affects their feelings of partnership.

- **Step 5 (Seek Common Ground and Compromise):** They agree on a weekly chore chart that divides tasks more equitably, acknowledging that adjustments may be needed.

- **Step 6 (Establish Agreements and Future Strategies):** They commit to a weekly check-in to discuss how the arrangement works and agree to approach future conflicts with the same steps to ensure both feel heard and valued.

Role-Play Scenario
Scenario for Practice: Taylor and Morgan have a recurring conflict about spending habits. Taylor, feeling anxious about finances, tends to be more frugal, while Morgan enjoys splurging on experiences and often dismisses Taylor's concerns, leading to repeated arguments.

Role-Play Exercise:
- **Step 1:** Taylor practices self-regulation techniques to calm financial anxiety before talking to Morgan.

- **Step 2:** Taylor initiates the conversation with, "I feel anxious when we spend a lot without discussing it first. I value our adventures together but want to feel secure in our financial future."

- **Step 3:** Morgan actively listens, summarizing Taylor's concerns and validating their feelings without agreement or defense.

- **Step 4:** Together, they focus on the issue—balancing enjoyment today with financial security for tomorrow—without attributing personal faults.

- **Step 5:** They brainstorm compromises, such as setting a monthly discretionary budget for spontaneity within limits.

- ***Step 6:*** They agree on a monthly plan to review their budget, discuss what's working and needs adjustment, and commit to using these conflict resolution steps in future disagreements.

By providing real-world examples and role-play scenarios, readers can see the conflict resolution process and practice the skills in a structured yet flexible context. This approach helps solidify the concepts and builds confidence in applying them to their relationships, offering a practical pathway toward healthier, more secure attachments.

Conclusion: The Growth Potential in Conflict

As we conclude our journey through the steps of constructive conflict resolution, it's vital to reflect on the profound potential for growth and deepening intimacy that mastering these skills offers. For individuals with anxious attachment, the transformation can be particularly significant, altering the very fabric of how they experience and navigate conflicts within their relationships.

Positive Framing: Conflict, often perceived with dread or anxiety, holds the seeds of growth and connection. By approaching disagreements with the mindset and strategies outlined, couples can turn moments of discord into opportunities for understanding, empathy, and, ultimately, deeper intimacy. This shift in perspective—from viewing conflict as a threat to seeing it as a catalyst for strengthening the bond—can dramatically change the dynamics of a relationship. It transforms the landscape from one of potential loss and fear to one of mutual growth and security.

The skills of self-regulation, active listening, validation, and compromise are not just tools for navigating conflict; they are expressions of love, respect, and commitment to the health and longevity of the relationship. By focusing on the issue rather than the person, seeking common ground, and establishing actionable agreements, couples can build a foundation of trust and understanding that withstands the inevitable challenges of sharing a life.

Continuous Practice: Developing these skills is a journey, not a destination. It requires patience, practice, and a willingness to learn from each interaction. The path is not always smooth; there will be missteps and challenges. However, each conflict presents a new opportunity to practice and refine these skills, deepen your understanding of yourself and your partner, and strengthen your relationship's fabric.

Encourage yourself and your partner to view each disagreement as a learning opportunity. Celebrate your progress, no matter how small, and remind each other of your shared commitment to growing together. The skills you develop through this process benefit your romantic relationship and can enhance your interactions with friends, family, and colleagues, enriching your emotional life.

In the end, the journey through conflict toward resolution is a powerful avenue for personal and relational growth. For those with anxious attachment, embracing these principles can be transformative, leading to relationships that are not only more secure but also more vibrant, fulfilling, and resilient. Remember, the goal is not to eliminate conflict but to learn to navigate it with grace, empathy, and understanding, turning challenges into opportunities for deeper connection and intimacy.

Chapter Exercises
"I Feel" Statements Exercise

Objective:

This exercise aims to enhance your communication skills, specifically in expressing feelings and needs effectively without assigning blame. Using 'I feel' statements allows for a more empathetic and understanding dialogue, fostering healthier and more constructive interactions.

Materials Needed:

- A notebook or digital device for recording your statements and reflections.
- A quiet space where you can think and reflect without interruptions.

Guide to Crafting "I Feel" Statements:

Step 1: Identify Your Feelings
Think about a recent situation where you experienced strong emotions. Focus on identifying exactly what you felt. Was it anger, sadness, frustration, or something else?

Step 2: Pinpoint the Cause
Reflect on what specifically triggered these feelings. Identify actions or circumstances rather than attributing your feelings to another person's character or intentions.

Step 3: Formulate Your "I Feel" Statement
Construct a sentence that begins with 'I feel' followed by your emotion, then describe the behavior or situation that led to this feeling. Avoid using 'you' in a way that sounds accusatory.

Step 4: Express Your Need
After expressing your feelings, describe what you need moving forward. This part of the statement should be actionable and focused on positive outcomes.

Step 5: Reflect on the Outcome
Consider how using 'I feel' statements might change the dynamics of your interactions. Reflect on how this expression makes you feel and how others might receive it.

Examples:

- **Before:** 'You never listen to me; you're always on your phone.'
- **After:** 'I feel ignored when talking and see you on your phone. I need us to be fully present during our conversations.'
- **Before**: 'You always leave the kitchen in a mess.'
- ***I feel*** overwhelmed when the kitchen is left untidy after cooking. I need help cleaning up so we can enjoy our meals and space together.'

Practice Scenario:

Imagine your partner forgot an important date that you had reminded them about.

- **Identify Your Feelings:** Disappointed, forgotten.
- **Pinpoint the Cause:** The importance of the date was overlooked despite reminders.
- **Formulate 'I Feel' Statement:** ' I feel disappointed and as though my needs were forgotten when our important date was overlooked, even after I mentioned how much it meant to me.'
- **Express Your Need:** *'I* need us to find a way to keep track of important dates together so we both feel valued and remembered.'

Conclusion:

The 'I Feel' Statements Exercise is valuable in cultivating open, blame-free communication. By focusing on expressing your feelings and needs, you create a space for understanding and empathy, paving the way for healthier, more supportive relationships.

Boundary Setting Workshop

Objective:

This workshop will help you identify and practice effectively communicating your boundaries to others. Understanding and asserting your boundaries is crucial for maintaining healthy relationships and self-respect.

Materials Needed:

- A notebook or digital device for note-taking.
- A quiet space for reflection and self-exploration.

Steps to Identify and Communicate Boundaries:

Step 1: Define Your Boundaries
Reflect on areas of your life where you need to set clear boundaries. These can include physical, emotional, intellectual, and spiritual boundaries. Write down what feels acceptable and what doesn't in these areas.

Step 2: Understand Your Needs
For each boundary you've identified, consider why it's important to you. What needs are these boundaries protecting? Understanding the 'why' behind your boundaries will help you communicate them more clearly.

Step 3: Practice Scripting
Create scripts for communicating your boundaries. Start your sentences with "I" to keep the focus on your feelings and needs. For example, "I feel overwhelmed when I don't have time to myself in the evenings. I need to establish a quiet hour for myself to recharge."

Step 4: Role Play
If possible, find a trusted friend or family member to practice with. Role-play scenarios where you need to assert your boundaries. Ask for feedback on your communication style and clarity.

Step 5: Reflect on Responses

After practicing, reflect on how it felt to state your boundaries. Consider what reactions you might encounter and how you will handle them while staying true to your needs.

Examples:

Physical Boundary: "I'm not comfortable with unsolicited physical contact. I need people to respect my personal space."

Emotional Boundary: "I feel drained when conversations are dominated by venting. I need to limit emotionally heavy discussions to times when we're both ready and willing to engage."

Intellectual Boundary: "I value respectful debates, but I need to step back when discussions become dismissive or heated."

Spiritual Boundary: "My spiritual beliefs are personal to me. I must share and explore these beliefs in environments that respect my perspective."

Conclusion:

Setting and communicating boundaries is an ongoing process that requires patience and practice. By clearly understanding your limits and needs, you can foster healthier interactions that respect your well-being and that of others. Remember, asserting your boundaries is not selfish—it's a fundamental aspect of self-care and respect.

Understanding without Agreeing with Exercise

Objective:

This exercise aims to enhance your communication skills by encouraging you to engage in discussions to understand another's point of view, even if you don't agree. It's about fostering empathy, deepening connections, and appreciating diverse perspectives.

Materials Needed:

- An open mind and willingness to listen.

- A journal or digital device to reflect on your experiences.
- A partner or friend willing to participate in the exercise with you.

Steps to Foster Understanding:

Step 1: Choose a Topic
Select a topic that you and your discussion partner have differing views on. It should be meaningful but not so contentious that it could harm your relationship.

Step 2: Set Ground Rules
Agree to listen actively and speak openly, with the intention of understanding rather than convincing. No interruptions or judgments are allowed.

Step 3: Share Perspectives
Take turns sharing your viewpoints on the topic. When it's your turn to listen, focus solely on understanding the other person's perspective. Ask clarifying questions if needed, but refrain from rebutting or debating their points.

Step 4: Reflect on What You Heard
After both have been shared, each person should summarize their perspective to ensure it's understood correctly. This isn't about agreement but ensuring accurate comprehension.

Step 5: Journal Your Reflections
Write about the experience in your journal. How did it feel to listen with the intention of understanding? Were there moments you struggled not to argue or defend your viewpoint? What did you learn about the other person's perspective and your listening skills?

Step 6: Discuss the Experience
Share your reflections. Discuss how the exercise impacted your view of the topic and whether it changed your feelings about future discussions.

Example:
Topic: The role of technology in children's lives.

- **Your Perspective:** Concerns about screen time and social isolation.
- **Their Perspective:** Belief in the educational benefits and connectivity technology offers.

Reflection: "Listening without arguing was challenging, especially when I strongly disagreed. However, I gained insight into their fears and hopes regarding technology, which I hadn't fully appreciated before. It reminded me that our ultimate goals are similar, even if our methods differ."

Conclusion:

The 'Understanding without Agreeing' exercise is a powerful tool for enhancing empathy and communication skills. By practicing active listening and seeking to understand rather than convince, you can build stronger, more respectful relationships and appreciate the rich diversity of human perspectives.

The Perspective Shift Exercise

Objective:

This transformative exercise is designed to cultivate empathy and deepen your understanding of others by exploring conflicts from their point of view. It challenges you to step outside your own experiences and consider someone else's feelings, thoughts, and motivations during a disagreement.

Materials Needed:

- A quiet space conducive to reflection and empathy.
- A journal or digital device for writing your perspective shift narrative.

Embracing Another's Viewpoint:

Step 1: Recall a Conflict
Think back to a recent conflict or disagreement you had with someone. It could be a partner, family member, colleague, or friend. Choose a situation that still feels unresolved or continues to affect you emotionally.

Step 2: Describe the Conflict
Briefly outline the conflict from your perspective first. What was the disagreement about? What emotions did you feel? What was your stance, and why did you feel justified in it?

Step 3: Shift Perspectives
Now, take a deep breath and consciously shift your viewpoint to that of the other person involved. Consider their possible emotions, thoughts, and motivations during the conflict. Write about the disagreement again, but this time, from their perspective. Strive for neutrality and empathy, avoiding assumptions or judgments.

Step 4: Identify New Insights
After writing the conflict from the other person's perspective, reflect on any new insights or understandings you gained. Did you discover potential reasons for their behavior that you hadn't considered before? How might their feelings have influenced the situation?

Step 5: Consider Solutions
With these new insights in mind, think about possible solutions or resolutions to the conflict that could be acceptable to both parties. Knowing what you do, how might you approach a conversation about this conflict now?

Example:

Original Perspective: "I was frustrated because my partner didn't help with household chores, even after I asked multiple times. It felt like they didn't respect my time or effort."

Shifted Perspective: "From my partner's viewpoint, they were overwhelmed with work deadlines and stressed about an upcoming project. They might have felt guilty for not contributing more at home but were too anxious to express it effectively."

New Insights: "I realize now that their lack of help wasn't about disrespect but rather their stress and poor communication. Perhaps I could have approached the conversation with more understanding of their work pressure."

Considered Solutions: "A solution might involve setting aside time to openly discuss our schedules and stressors, to distribute household tasks more equitably based on our current capacities."

Conclusion:

The Perspective Shift Exercise offers a powerful means to foster relationship empathy and understanding. By intentionally adopting another's viewpoint, you can uncover new pathways to resolution and deepen your connections with others. This practice not only aids in resolving conflicts but also enriches your emotional intelligence and relational skills.

Jealousy Journaling Exercise

Objective:

This exercise is designed to help you navigate feelings of jealousy by journaling. It's a tool to explore and understand the underlying fears and insecurities that often fuel these feelings, aiming to foster self-awareness and emotional growth.

Materials Needed:

- A journal or any digital writing device.
- A quiet and comfortable space for reflection.

Embrace the Process:

Step 1: Notice and Acknowledge
Whenever you feel jealousy creeping into your thoughts, could you take a moment to acknowledge it? Recognize that jealousy is a natural emotion that can offer insights into deeper aspects of your emotional landscape.

Step 2: Journal the Experience
Write about the incident that triggered your jealousy as soon as possible. Describe the situation, including who was involved, what happened, and how you reacted internally and externally.

Step 3: Reflect on Underlying Causes
After detailing the incident, delve into what you believe are the underlying reasons for your jealousy. Are you feeling insecure about yourself or the relationship? Is there a fear of loss or inadequacy lurking beneath? Try to be as honest with yourself as possible.

Step 4: Explore Your Feelings

Expand on how the jealousy made you feel. Beyond the surface emotion of jealousy, are there feelings of anger, sadness, or fear? Identifying these can help you address the issue's root rather than just the symptoms.

Step 5: Identify Needs and Desires

Consider what jealousy signals about your needs and desires in the relationship or within yourself. Perhaps you're seeking reassurance, more open communication, or a need to feel valued and heard.

Step 6: Plan Constructive Actions

Based on your reflections, think of constructive actions you can take to address these underlying needs and insecurities. This might involve honest conversation with your partner, working on your self-esteem, or setting boundaries.

Examples:

Situation: You felt jealous when your partner was talking and laughing with someone else at a party.

Underlying Cause: Fear of being less interesting or engaging than others.

Feelings: Insecurity, sadness, fear of being inadequate.

Needs/Desires: Need for reassurance from your partner about your value in the relationship.

Action Plan: Communicate your feelings to your partner, expressing the need for reassurance without accusing them of wrongdoing.

Step 7: Reflect on Your Growth

Regularly revisit your journal entries to reflect on your growth. Over time, you may notice patterns in what triggers your jealousy and how you learn to cope more healthily.

Conclusion:

Jealousy journaling is a powerful exercise for uncovering the fears and insecurities that often lie beneath the surface of our emotional reactions. By engaging in this practice, you can better understand yourself and your relationships, paving the way for emotional resilience and more secure connections.

Made in the USA
Columbia, SC
20 September 2024